the
LIBRARY
of
DREAMS

ALSO BY HOWARD SCHWARTZ

POETRY
Vessels
Gathering the Sparks
Sleepwalking Beneath the Stars
Breathing in the Dark

FICTION
A Blessing Over Ashes
Midrashim
The Captive Soul of the Messiah
Rooms of the Soul
Adam's Soul
The Four Who Entered Paradise

AS EDITOR
Imperial Messages: One Hundred Modern Parables
Voices Within the Ark: The Modern Jewish Poets
Gates to the New City: A Treasury of Modern Jewish Tales
The Dream Assembly: Tales of Rabbi Zalman Schachter-Shalomi
Elijah's Violin & Other Jewish Fairy Tales
Miriam's Tambourine: Jewish Tales from Around the World
Lilith's Cave: Jewish Tales of the Supernatural
Gabriel's Palace: Jewish Mystical Tales
Tree of Souls: The Mythology of Judaism
Leaves from the Garden of Eden: One Hundred Classic Jewish Tales

ESSAYS
Reimagining the Bible: The Storytelling of the Rabbis

FOR CHILDREN
The Diamond Tree
The Sabbath Lion
Next Year in Jerusalem
The Wonder Child
A Coat for the Moon
Ask the Bones
A Journey to Paradise
The Day the Rabbi Disappeared
Invisible Kingdoms
Before You Were Born
More Bones
Gathering Sparks

the
LIBRARY
of
DREAMS

NEW & SELECTED POEMS 1965-2013

HOWARD SCHWARTZ

ART BY CAREN LOEBEL-FRIED

 BkMk Press
University of Missouri-Kansas City

BkMk Press
University of Missouri-Kansas City
5101 Rockhill Road
Kansas City, Missouri 64110
(816) 235-2558 (voice) / (816) 235-2611 (fax)
www.umkc.edu/bkmk

Financial assistance for this project has been provided by the
Missouri Arts Council, a state agency.

Book design: Susan L. Schurman
Managing editor: Ben Furnish
Executive editor: Robert Stewart

BkMk Press wishes to thank Taylor Wallace, Grace Stansberry,
Marie Mayhugh.

Printing by Walsworth Publishing Co., Marceline, Mo.

Library of Congress Cataloging-in-Publication Data

Schwartz, Howard, 1945-
The Library of Dreams : New & Selected Poems 1965-2013 / Howard Schwartz.
Kansas City, MO : BkMk Press-University of Missouri-Kansas City, 2013.
p. cm.
ISBN: 9781886157880 (paperback : alk. paper)
Summary: "These poems explore subjects drawn from the Hebrew Bible
and Jewish mysticism as well as contemporary Jewish American life and
imagination"-- Provided by publisher.
PS3569.C5657 L53 2013
811/.54   2013019630

This book is set in Dante and Charlemegne.

ACKNOWLEDGMENTS

Some of the poems included here have been reprinted from the following:

BOOKS
Vessels (Greensboro, NC: Unicorn Press, 1977).
Gathering the Sparks (St. Louis, MO: Singing Wind Press, 1979).
Sleepwalking Beneath the Stars (Kansas City, MO: BkMk Press, 1992).
Breathing in the Dark (Saginaw, MI: Mayapple Press, 2011).

CHAPBOOKS
Signs of the Lost Tribe (Tuscaloosa, AL: Accidental Balestra Press, 1994).
A Shelter of Stars (Venice, CA: Shulamis Press, 2006).

JOURNALS
Ars Interpres: "Fable of the Bird"
Blue Lyra Review: "The Angel of Ripeness."
The Forward: "Yehuda Amichai in the Heavenly Jerusalem," "The First Eve,"
    "The Fiery Serpents," and "The Angel of Losses."
Focus/Midwest: "Gifts" (an earlier version).
Handbook: "A Song."
The Jewish Advocate: "Antidotes."
Judaism: "Gathering the Sparks" and "Abraham in Egypt."
Kerem: "Manna," "The Spice of the Sabbath," and "Genealogy."
The Literary Review: "Calling the Moon Closer," "The Eve," and "Winter
    Harvest."
Maggid: "My Father Had Many Professions."
Maitrea: "Moontide."
The Midwest Quarterly: "A Shelter of Stars."
Minnesota Review: "Lullaby," "The Twin," "The Trapped," and "Dream Palm"
Moonstone: "Lost Myth of Albashad."
Natural Bridge: "Retirement."
New Letters: "The Sound of Tearing," "In That Country," "Dream Child,"
    "The Last Reading, "The Last Time I Saw Lilith," "A Palace of Bird
    Beaks, " and "A Bamboo Flute."
New Vilna Review: "Swimming to Jerusalem" and "Dream Visit."
The New York Quarterly: "Adam's Dream."
Panjandrum Poetry Journal: "Sarah" and "Oracle."
PoetryMagazine.com: "New Skin,"
River Styx: "Salt," "Mississippi John Hurt Buried in the Pepper," and "Tribe of
    the Jewelers."
The Sagarin Review: "A Wall Rubbing," "Signs of the Lost Tribe," "The
    Tomb of the Ari," and "The Last Sunset."
St. Louis Post-Dispatch: "Breathing in the Dark."

Studies in American Jewish Literature: "The Minyan."
Webster Review: "The Prayers," "In the Ancient Days," and "Our Angels,"
Zeek: "Dreams About Kafka."

ANTHOLOGIES

Contemporary Missouri Authors: "Tribe of the Jewelers"
The Bloomsburg Anthology of Contemporary Jewish Poetry: "Breathing in
        the Dark," "Signs of the Lost Tribe," and "In That Country."
Dancing at the Edge of the World: "Our Angels."
Dr. Generosity's Almanac: "The Twin."
First Harvest: Jewish Writing in St. Louis 1991-1997: "A Wall Rubbing,"
        "The Last Sunset," and "The Tribe of the Jewelers."
Five Missouri Poets: "Psalm," "These Two," and "Antidotes."
Flood Stage: An Anthology of St. Louis Poets: "Signs of the Lost Tribe," and
        "Sleepwalking Beneath the Stars."
Forms of Prayer for Jewish Worship: "In the Ancient Days."
Heartland II: Poets of the Midwest: "Love Poem."
How to Eat a Poem: "Vessels."
Jewish American Poetry: Poems, Commentary and Reflections: "Signs of
        the Lost Tribe."
The Jewish Book of Days: "Gathering the Sparks."
*Memories and Memoirs: Essays, Poems, Stories and Letters by Contemporary
        Missouri Authors:* "Tribe of the Jewelers."
Mishkan T'filah: A Reform Siddur for the House of Mourning: "Our Angels."
New Harvest: Jewish Writing in St. Louis 1998-2005: "Waking Too Late,"
        "The First Eve," "Out of Egypt," and "Yehuda Amichai in the Heavenly
        Jerusalem."
Sacred Therapy: "Gathering the Sparks."
Seder Tu Bishevat: "The Festival of Trees" and "The New Year for Trees."
Tambourine: "Lullaby."
Voices from the Interior: "Our Angels," "Blessing of the Firstborn," and
        "Iscah."
Voices Within the Ark: The Modern Jewish Poets: "Our Angels," "Gather-
        ing the Sparks," "Adam's Dream," "Abraham in Egypt," "Iscah,"
        "The New Year for Trees," "The Prayers," "Vessels," "A Song,"
        "These Two," "Blessing of the Firstborn," "Shira," and "Psalm."
Winter Harvest: Jewish Writing in St. Louis, 2006-2011: "Inheritance," "A
        Portrait of My Son," "Spirit Guide," and "Feathers."

AS SONGS

"These Two" music by Georgia Stitt.
"A Song," music by Stanley Hoffman.
"Oracle of the Oil," music by Laura Fishman.

BOOK FOR CHILDREN

Before You Were Born (Roaring Book Press).

THE LIBRARY OF DREAMS

I. THE LIBRARY OF DREAMS (2013)

II Breathing in the Dark (2011)

III Sleepwalking Beneath the Stars (1992)

IV Gathering the Sparks (1979)

V Vessels (1977)

For Tsila,
Shira
Nati
Miriam
Ari
and Ava

I

THE LIBRARY OF DREAMS

(2013)

GENEALOGY

In the beginning I was a swirl of dust
carried by cosmic winds.
I couldn't hear the silence.
I couldn't see the stars circling around me.
I was entirely turned within,
focused on a holy spark,
a cosmic seed waiting to be sown
in a palace of its own creation.

It took a long time
before my eyes opened.
Who knows how long?
By then the holy seed had taken root
inside me,
giving me the blessing of breath,
and guiding me
out of darkness
as I crawled into the unknown.

I learned how the river lifts with rain,
and how to draw my breath back and forth
through countless stars.
I can still recall
all the prior worlds I passed through
to reach this instant, alive.
Even now a vibrating reed of breath
shelters me in a house of song.

COLLECTORS

in memory of Gabriel Preil

The collector of caves makes his way in the dark
to discover
every hidden passage.

The collector of maps
holds the world
in his hands.

The collector of autumns
cherishes every leaf
that falls.

The collector of sunsets
has sworn
never to forget.

The collector of covenants
puts up tents in the wilderness
and counts the stars.

MANNA

The people went around gathering it.
—Num. 11:8

for Jeff Friedman

Every morning
we crawl out of our tents
and make our way into the desert,
each in his own direction,
to gather words
fallen overnight
from heaven.

Some rise even earlier,
before dawn,
to catch the words as they drift down,
believing words caught in this way
are more potent
than those gathered
where they fell.

Some days we come back
with an armful of possibilities,
some days with only a few scattered words
that refuse to reveal their meaning.
Even then we scrutinize them,
rearranging them endlessly,
hoping to discern their mystery.

We depend on this heavenly beneficence
to sustain us. Without it,
the desert would be barren,
our lives unbearable.
Above all, we relish the double portion
that falls before the Sabbath
to keep us during our day of rest.

THE IMMORTALS

for Cherie Karo Schwartz

Long ago they abandoned the heavens
and descended to the world below
as white owls.

Hidden from sight,
they peer out from the branches
and trace the winding path of every being.

During the day they observe the world unseen;
at night they feast on forgotten memories
and reply to unasked questions.

For them nothing is wasted,
nothing passes without being seized,
nothing is ignored.

Without them,
the past would be erased at sunset,
and a long silence would descend on our lives.

DOLPHIN SONGS

in memory of Donald Finkel

No one remembers how long ago
they abandoned the land
and embraced the sea,
or why—
were they were driven out
by floods or hostile tribes,
or did they set out to explore
the deep?

In this new world where waves ruled,
there was no way to pass down their lore
but in song.
Therefore they sing to each other
in clicks and whistles
and beautiful long breaths,
recalling their myths one by one,
until every dolphin knows them by heart.

What are those songs about?
Do they celebrate leaving the land,
or mourn their exile from it?
Are their myths of mermaids
and sirens
and heroic rescues?
Or do they chant psalms and prayers
in praise of the sea?

And are we so different?
Myths lead us through many mirrors
to find ourselves, preserve our childhood
in their amber jewels, hide
our oldest memories
in their secret caves, peer
into the future
through their crystal balls.

LANGUAGES

Deep calls unto deep.
—Psalms 42:8.

Everything has its own language—
a star sends its message at the speed of light,
although it may take centuries
to reach us.

A tree is not as silent as you may think.
When the wind sways its branches,
the tree sighs
in its own language.

The sea speaks in its own tongue,
reciting the poems
the moon calls forth.

Even the dead,
speechless so long,
have their own language,
and when their silence calls out to us,
we listen.

THE MYTH OF MYSELF

Everyone has a myth,
a personal myth.
All these years I've been searching
for mine.
I studied paintings in caves,
carvings on trees,
maps of the stars.

I looked in books of myth and magic,
in ancient teachings
and spells,
in dolphin songs
and silences,
in breathing,
and in holding my breath.

Yes, I found fragments scattered
like clues,
but I had never been able
to piece them together.
So late one night
I called upon the immortals to guide me,
and they led me to the library of dreams.

Surrounded by an infinity of shelves,
I picked out a book at random.
There, in fiery letters,
was the myth I had sought so long.
As I read it, I lived it,
following the path burned into my being
before I was born.

THE ANGEL OF RIPENESS

While she waits for the sun
to bestow its blessing,
she rocks the cradle
back and forth,
tending the seed
the way a cloud and river
nurture the rain.

Every grain in the field,
every grape on the vine,
even the moon
listens
to the song she hums
under her breath.

HER PALETTE

for Marjorie Stelmach

Sometimes she peers out her window
so long,
she takes leave of her body
and gives herself to the winds,
no longer a witness,
but a being begotten
in the image of God.

While the one inside the house
reads her way through libraries,
or meditates on mysteries of origins
and endings,
the one sailing in the wind rejoices,
free of the shadow of doubt.

When she comes back
from these secret journeys,
she brings a shimmering vision with her
fragile as a rope of wind,
and drawing on the elements
of creation,
she brings splendid new poems into being.

THE INTERPRETER

While others hear a language without words,
he hears the confessions
of the composer,
the violin maker,
and the player,
all at the same time.

Everywhere he goes
unknown tongues seek him out—
the languages of the birds, the winds, the rain,
but who can he tell?
Although he can comprehend
every whisper,
he has no language of his own
in which to share it.

If he could only reveal these mysteries to others,
they would understand—
the only silence
is the one they insist
on not hearing.

LEGACY

I spent many lifetimes
watching the moon grow full

before it diminished
and disappeared.

I found shelter in trees
late at night,

and learned the language of longing
from the leaves.

I saw how seeds sprouted,
how blossoms broke open,

how leaves became beautiful
before abandoning their branches.

I never grew tired of the sound of water
creating its own silence.

These are the languages I count on
to reveal their mysteries,

secrets accrued over the ages,
resonant with meaning.

FABLE OF THE BIRD

This is the bird that invented silence.
She created it one day
when she stopped
singing.

If you listen carefully when the wind dies down
you can hear her silent
song.

When the silence has lasted too long,
she breaks it in two

and invents it
all over
again.

THIS HOUSE

I inherited this house.
It suits me perfectly, for as I change,
it changes.
As a child I was only aware
of my bedroom and backyard,
but as I grew older I discovered new rooms—
an attic filled with stacks of books,
a bedroom with a window to the stars,
a darkroom,
a wine cellar,
a basement full of mysteries.

I've lost the key
to the room of my mother's dreams,
so it remains locked.
My father's room is filled with broken watches
he intended to fix.
It, too, is locked.
There's a small synagogue,
with its own Ark,
a place of refuge,
and a spacious study
where I long to write.

Did I mention the foundation?
It consists entirely of rubble.

DREAM JOURNEYS

I wander all night in my vision.
—Walt Whitman

All night
we drift back and forth
on a sea of dreams,
floating from one world to the next.
There we lead alternate lives,
live in different homes,
with different mates
and different children.

In these dream worlds
the dead seem perfectly alive.
It's here they meet
with the living
to share family secrets.
In one dream my grandfather,
long gone, tells me
what spirits have access to the past,
but not the future.

Before waking,
I pour a glass for you
from a clear pitcher
where my dreams have been
preserved.

THE DREAMER

for Henry Shapiro

He is the real artist,
embracing emotions
and weaving them into dreams.
His myth is memory,
his religion, return,
the only torch he carries,
an abandoned map.

Icy forms, envious gods of silence,
try to capture his creations
before they can escape.
The traitor posted on the narrow bridge
between sleeping and waking
insists that everything
be left behind.

Still his voice grows inside me—
holding one word
between two breaths
like a long note,
he descends into sleep.
There he mines himself for diamonds,
hard to find.

THE LAST READING

in memory of Donald Finkel

Don,
you were always exploring
caves,
glaciers,
mysterious voyages,
lame angels,
and every manner of beast.
Every two years
a new book of yours appeared,
full of surprises. You were famous,
or as you put it,
A high little star provoketh wonder.

One night I took a walk
and found myself in front of your house.
I wanted to visit, but was afraid
you might be writing a poem,
or making love with your wife.

Years later,
as we sat together in my car,
I told you my fantasy of teaching
where you did.
Your reply:
Baby, they'd tear you to pieces.

You were planning to move.
I asked why. You said,
*I've written all the poems I can
from that house.*

Then came retirement, the move,

and a series of catastrophes—
your beloved Connie gone,
your publisher lost,
your books pulped,
your memory starting to betray you.

Yet even without a wife, a publisher,
or a neighborhood of friends,
you still wrote—
your last poems among your best.
Your last reading,
at Left Bank Books,
was crowded with friends.
Although you could barely read,
a cat saved the day—
coming up and rubbing against you,
and you picked it up and stroked it,
and nothing else mattered.

GRANDFATHERS

in memory of William Rubin and Charles Schwartz

Both escaped the Tsar's army
and left Russia behind.
One smuggled his brother out.
The other
abandoned a wife and two children,
and married a girl of sixteen
right off the boat.

I remember sitting on that grandfather's knee,
listening to *Gang Busters*.
No one was allowed to talk
when that came on.
The other loved to watch boxing on TV,
thrusting his arms
at an invisible adversary.

Like my mother's father,
I struggle with ghosts.
Like my father's father,
I can't resist a compelling tale.
Like both of them,
I'm always at the border,
determined to escape.

GREBENES

in memory of Lena Schwartz

She was the last of her sisters to cross the ocean,
arriving at sixteen,
soon to be wed.
I never knew her then, although I saw her photograph.
I only knew my ancient Grandma,
who always looked old.

Everyone knew she was a master of making
gefilte fish—a secret recipe
she refused to share with my mother.
She let me play with raw liver,
so spongy, and fed me chicken feet
and *grebenes*—chicken skin fried to a crisp.

Of course she kept kosher.
I was there when she purified pots and pans,
planting them in the backyard
for three days,
then digging them up
and using them again.

We lived next door. I went back and forth
through the hole in the fence all day long.
There was one television in the family,
in my parents' bedroom.
She watched every night till it signed off.
My mother never forgave her.

IF I COME BACK

I'll return again,
as a snake or a raucous bird,
or, with luck, as a lion.
 —Theodore Roethke

If I come back as a firefly,
will I remember how high I used to swing
in the dark?

If I come back as a butterfly,
will I remember breathing in the scent
of lilacs?

If I come back as a spider,
will I remember hiding from my sister
under the porch?

If I come back as a bee,
will I remember searching
for a four-leaf clover?

If I come back as a sparrow,
will I remember the delicious grapes
from my grandfather's vines?

If I come back as a turtle,
will I remember how I loved the taste
of strawberries?

If I come back as a rabbit,
will I remember the carrots I planted
in the backyard?

If I come back as an owl,
will I remember how high I climbed

in that tree?

If I come back as a puppy,
will I remember the puppies
my father brought home in his pockets?

If I come back as a kitten,
will I remember my kitten,
asleep at the foot of my bed?

THE LOST FILM

A year before I was born,
my family gathered in the backyard,
wearing their finest clothes,
to be filmed by cousin Benny.
That brief glimpse into the past,
lost for so long,
has just made its way to me.

Halfway through the silent film,
Ida, my father's sister,
appears with her husband, Sam.
My father and mother are next to appear,
newly married,
radiating youth.
My mother, twenty, and exceptionally beautiful,
my father, twenty-seven,
muscular, handsome and confident.
I'm willing to bet
the suit he's wearing was his wedding suit.
The other men are dressed as soldiers.

In the next scene
my father jokes with Maury,
his younger brother,
the only one in the film still living.

Last to appear are my grandparents.
She peers at the camera
as if this were the first time
she had seen one.
He hides coyly behind the porch post,
then peeks out,

steps into the yard,
and comes very close to the camera,
looking exactly as I remember him.

Everyone in the family
is there,
except me.
No one seems to have noticed
I'm missing.

DREAMS ABOUT MY FATHER

1. Dream Journey

My father and I start out on a journey,
but when we have only crossed
the yard,
he decides to turn back.
He says, *It's time to make a fresh start.*
I argue,
but he takes a shovel
and covers his footprints
with dirt.

2. Riding a Horse

I go out in the backyard.
My father appears, riding a horse.
He seems distracted
and doesn't notice me.
Instead, he rides around the yard
in a circle.

3. Photos from the Future

I fly back into the past
over a beautiful body of water, dark colors
of purple and blue. When I arrive,
I meet my father as a young man.
I show him photos of our family
in the future.
He finds it hard to believe,
but a photo of his mother looking much older
convinces him.

4. A Gift

My father says,
Come down to the basement,
I have something to show you.
I hurry down.
He hands me a small wooden box,
with a candle in each corner,
holding a miniature scroll of the Torah.
I've been saving this for you.

5. Horse and Carriage

The backyard behind our house is muddy
and partly flooded. My father appears,
swimming, and uses a cow
to pull out a horse and carriage
stuck in the mud.
The effort is exhausting,
the water high, the mud treacherous.
I watch him catch his breath,
and prepare to swim after him
if he slips under.

6. Melting Snow

As my father and I walk home together,
he tells me how hard his life has become,
how much time it takes to earn a living,
how many years since he bought a new pair of socks.
And all the while I'm aware
that each of his steps
seems to sink in the earth,
as if he were walking on melting snow.

6. The Silver Tree

Not long before he died,
my father told me this dream:
A silver tree had taken root
outside our kitchen window,
its branches filled with silver fruit,
its trunk rising above the roof.
Dazed, he opened the door
and stepped out
into the silver shadow.

7. The Eve

My father dies on the eve of a Jewish holiday,
then comes back to life.
He's very calm
and surprised to see the tears in our eyes.
He says he's never felt better.
He gets up and we walk outside, feeling close.
The moon and stars pull us to them,
as if into an embrace.

WEIGHING GOLD

Knowing my father
wouldn't live long enough
to see my first book,
I showed him a book
of the same size,
and he closed his eyes,
weighing it in his hand,
the way he weighed gold.

I never felt closer to him.

A BAMBOO FLUTE

One night
I came upon a pavilion
filled with music.
Someone offered me an instrument,
and I chose a bamboo flute.
Though I couldn't play,
I brought the flute to my lips
and that same music flowed from me
as if I were the source.

All the dreams of childhood consumed me
while I played,
but when I paused for breath,
I found the flute had cracked.
Suddenly afraid,
I tried the flute once more,
and this time
the notes soared into the unknown,
and I became one with the flute.

Waking in the dream,
I ran to my father
to tell him of my gift.
He smiled and said, *I know.*

DREAMS ABOUT MY MOTHER

1. Transplanting a Tree

My mother has given me the job
of transplanting a huge, blossoming tree
from our backyard.
I manage to move it,
but there is much doubt
about whether or not
it will take root again.

2. The Room

She tells me her recurrent dream—
there's a room in our house
no one ever enters.
She peers through a little window
in the door,
but never steps inside.

3. Thirst

I see my mother kneeling by a lake,
filling a canteen,
sipping the water,
then pouring it over her face and body.
I can sense her thirst.

4. Relieving Pressure

My mother has been waiting for me
to relieve some pressure
on her shoulders,

using a method I've just learned.
The anticipation has made her calm,
and the method works.

5. A World of Dancers

I'm walking at night along a dark road
when I come to a cove, shaped like a half moon.
A great crowd has gathered there,
standing in endless lines.
I wander among them, mystified,
and almost fail to recognize my mother,
who tells me she's been waiting there for years
to obtain a release only given
every tenth year.
Now it's almost midnight of the new year,
and the line hasn't moved any closer.
Just then bells begin to chime,
and everyone, including my mother,
finds a partner and begins to dance.

LAST VISIT

in memory of my mother

For ten years
your memory
slipped away from you,
until almost nothing was left.

When we came to visit that night,
you sat up in bed,
and, for one evening,
lost memories of your family
found you,
and a light shone from your face—

the blessing of clarity
one last time.

ESCAPE ARTIST

for Tsila

My wife is an artist—
an escape artist.
You can find her in Prague,
Amsterdam,
Copenhagen,
or Berlin.
Even Houdini would admire her—
now you see her,
now you don't.
Only Jerusalem can hold her back.

There
she wanders the streets of the Old City
searching for her son,
our son,
who has also escaped.
But he knows
she will find him
no matter where he's hidden,
and that it's hopeless
to hide.

I wake here alone.
The walls are filled with her artwork,
but she's not here.
Jerusalem has prevailed.
And I know
that as soon as she comes back,
she'll be planning
her next escape.

MAURY HAS SLIPPED AWAY

in memory of Maury Schwartz

Maury has slipped away
from this world.
It was as sudden as a single breath.
Now four children gather
to see him
one last time.

With infinite patience,
his body lies on a table,
waiting for them—
his eyes closed,
his face radiant.

Even the line of his lips,
disfigured of late,
has been set free.

LITTLE BIRD

for Miriam

That summer in Jerusalem,
home of her mother's family,
she was another person,
waking early,
combing her hair to the other side,
planting a garden of possibilities.
One night
she heard a voice that had been hidden, saying,
Sing for me, my little bird,
sing for me your song.
So she sang and discovered
that long-silent voice
was her own.

It had ripened
by itself,
like the most delicious grapes.

THE FIRST BREATH

As the first to exist, God brought Himself into being.
—Ma'ayan Hokhmah

Longing to exist, God drew in
the first breath,
the whirlwind that created suns and moons,
gathering stars into galaxies,
bringing heaven and earth into being.

Some say that long breath is eternal,
and this cauldron of stars was created
out of a single breath.
Others say a time may come
when this world will be uncreated
till God draws another breath.

There's another interpretation,
rarely stated, often hinted at—
that God is dreaming this world
and everything in it—
and all existence depends on how long
that dream lasts.

ADAM'S SOUL

All souls were included in Adam's soul.
—Exodus Rabbah

Before God created Adam
as a man of flesh and blood,
he created a dream Adam.

God called forth this dream Adam and said:
Alone among all my creations,
I am going to permit you to choose your own soul.

And God brought Adam to the treasury of souls.
When Adam looked inside,
he saw a sky crowded with stars.

And God said:
Every one of those stars is a soul.
Which one do you want?

Now every star glowed with a light of its own.
Every one was equally beautiful.
Which one should he choose?

Then Adam saw that the constellation of stars
formed a great tree of souls,
branching out in every direction.

And Adam replied to God and said:
I want the soul of the tree of souls,
from which all souls are suspended.

God was delighted,
and brought forth that soul
and gave it to Adam.

That's why the soul of Adam
contains all souls, and why all souls
are but a part of Adam's soul.

GIFTS

When she brought me a fig,
I reminded her
it was a forbidden fruit.

When she brought me a mandrake root,
I left it out in the sun to dry,
so it could serve as a charm
between two bodies,
binding one root
to another.

When she brought me a pomegranate,
we devoured it
without wasting a single seed.

THE TREE OF LIFE AND
THE TREE OF DEATH

I put you in the Garden of Eden
so you would eat from the tree of life.
—Midrash Tanhuma

Yes, there was a test,
but not the one you think,
the one recounted in Genesis.

Yes, there were two trees,
but knowledge of good and evil
had nothing to do with it.

Like any parent,
He wanted the best for His children,
but they had to make the decision themselves.

So He gave them a hint:
Pssst—Don't eat of the tree of death.
But of course they did.

That's why He put two angels
at the gates of Eden,
to guard the way to the tree of life.

His children have never forgiven him.

A WANDERING SOUL

All at once
a spirit descending from above
reaches you,
a wandering soul waiting
to be born.

She first appears
as a young girl
bringing you a prayer book,
a ribbon marking the place
she wants you to read.
Later
she comes back
as a bride.

If you open the door,
you could bring her
into being—
a woman
bearing the image of a goddess,
with a full moon
resting
in her hands.

BEFORE YOU WERE BORN

for Ari and Ava

Before you were born,
your soul made its home in the highest heaven,
in the treasury of souls.
The angel Lailah watched over you.
One day a heavenly voice went forth,
announcing to all the angels
that the time had come for you to be born.
Then the angel Lailah led your soul
out of the treasury of souls,
and brought you down to this world.

Once you were here,
Lailah told your soul to enter a seed.
Then Lailah brought that seed to your mother,
and you started to grow inside her.
While you were growing,
Lailah lit a lamp inside your mother's womb
and read to you from the book of mysteries.
As you slept, Lailah taught you
all the secrets in the world.
She taught you seventy languages,
including the languages of all the animals.
She even taught you the language of the wind.
So too did she tell you the history of your soul,
and reveal the past and future to you.
And even though you were asleep,
you listened with delight
to all she had to say.

Finally,
the time came for you to be born.
Then the angel Lailah led you out into the world.

But the moment you were born,
Lailah put her finger to your lips, reminding you
to keep everything secret.
That's how you got the indentation
on your upper lip.
It's your reminder of all Lailah taught you
before you were born—

and all you have forgotten.

THE GOLEM SPEAKS

for Steve Stern

I know that at any moment
I could return to dust.
Mute since my creation,
I am forbidden to write,
sing,
or make love.

Yet my hands are full of questions,
my eyes take in everything.
I refuse to be dragged into the swamp
of forgetting,
into quicksands
of all I have abandoned.

I, too, have secrets.
I, too, inhale
and exhale
the breath of life.
I, too, was created
in the image of God.

Every life is sacred—
even mine.

THE LAST TIME I SAW LILITH

Out Lilith!
—Sefer Raziel

Lilith chases desire—
she doesn't knock, she lets herself in.
If the door doesn't open,
she slides beneath it like a shadow
and slips under the sheets.
She's not always unwelcome.

For many years
she made her home
in my cellar.
She beckoned
late at night,
when everyone else was asleep.

Many nights I felt her long hair
brushing my face
as I drifted into sleep.
I tried not to think about the sons
she would give birth to,
half human, half demon.

The last time I saw Lilith
she did not seem as stunning.
She had slung her mattress
over her shoulder,
and she was on her way
out.

ABRAHAM'S TENT

for Eve Ilsen

Eve said:
Close your eyes
and imagine you're in Abraham's tent,
open on all sides,
peering out into the distance.
What do you see?

I closed my eyes
and saw myself
peering out of the tent, waiting.

All at once
three travelers swept in,
filling the tent with primordial light—
and for a few instants,
I experienced
eternity.

Then the tent disappeared,
and I was back in the room
with Eve,
my eyes opened.

A DREAM OF WORSHIP

I find myself on a distant island,
where I've come to worship Abraham.
I'm preparing a sacrifice for him.
I join a long line of worshipers
outside a cave
waiting for the ceremony to begin.
An old woman seated on black stone
blesses me as I pass by.

Inside, a young woman lights the fire.
She's clear about her role,
but I'm not about mine—
how to pause between two breaths,
how to lie down in darkness
and measure
a minute of death.

THE SPICE OF THE SABBATH

for Rabbi Jim Bennett

Despite what you may have heard,
Abraham and Sarah never died.
They were rewarded with eternal life
in the Garden of Eden—
they've lived there
ever since they took leave of this world.

During the week
Abraham wanders in the garden,
gathering dry leaves in a basket.
On the eve of the Sabbath,
Sarah crushes those leaves
and casts their powder into the winds.

Then the winds,
guided by angels,
carry the powder to the four corners of the earth,
so that all those who breathe in
even the smallest speck
have a taste of paradise.

WHY IS ISAAC MISSING?

Abraham then returned to his servants,
and they departed together for Beersheva.
—Genesis 22:19

for Marc Bregman

When it was all over,
Abraham came down the mountain,
alone.
Watching from a great distance,
we wonder,
why is Isaac missing?

Some say that when the knife touched Isaac's throat,
his soul took flight,
ascending to the palaces of heaven.

Others say Isaac was so terrified,
that when Abraham unbound him,
he ran away, found shelter
with his brother, Ishmael,
and never returned to the father
who was ready to slay him
at the whim of an invisible god.
After that,
Isaac rarely lifted his eyes
to heaven.

We hear nothing more of Isaac
until he was a blind old man,
tricked into believing his son, Jacob,
was his firstborn, Esau.

Neither rabbis nor storytellers
could explain that gulf, that lacuna
in his life, all those years
Isaac was missing.

JACOB NEVER DIED

Everyone thought that Jacob had died.
Surrounded by his sons,
he gave his final blessings,
and his soul departed.
No matter,
Jacob never died.

He was present during the Exodus,
witnessed the crossing of the Red Sea
and the drowning of Pharaoh's army.
So too did he witness the giving of the Torah,
the ascent of Elijah,
and Daniel's encounter with the dragon Bel.
He alone lived to see the Temple built,
destroyed,
and rebuilt.

Some say he is still with us,
watching over his descendants.
Others say Jacob lives on
in his seed.

PEOPLE OF THE STORIES

*I am hearing the words of the Torah
as they were spoken at Sinai.*
　　　—Ben Azzai

for Rabbi Lane and Linda Steinger

Wherever we wander,
we take our stories with us,
following invisible paths into the past,
searching for the tents of Jacob.
Long before they were written down,
these myths
were burned into memory
where past and present
intermingle.

There Adam and Eve
can still be found in the garden,
Noah in the ark,
and Abraham's still counting stars.
Isaac lies bound and terrified on the altar,
Jacob still wrestles with the angel,
Joseph's still in the pit,
and Moses is still on Mount Sinai,
receiving the Torah.

We repeat these stories every day
and relive them in dreams at night.
In return, they shelter us
in the very tents
we are seeking,
where Abraham and Sarah are still alive,
Jacob never died,
and it's still possible to meet them
in this world or the next.

I BREATHED IN

for Deena

I breathed in
to make space for you
in my life.

The sky,
empty so long,
filled with stars,
wind embraced the branches,
a full moon rose
from where it was hidden.

I breathed out a long sigh.
There was room enough
for us both.

THE CALLING

One night
the Ari heard a voice
calling out to him.
But as soon as he opened the door,
he was swept up by celestial currents,
carried across the heavens,
and brought back
to the very beginning.

There he saw ten vessels of light,
indescribably beautiful,
sail forth out of the darkness.
Each held the promise of perfection,
but then they shattered,
scattering holy sparks
into every corner
of creation.

That's when
the Ari grasped his purpose
and that of his people—
to gather those sparks,
so that the repair of the worlds
above
and below
could commence.

His disciple, Israel Sarug,
comments:
It should be the aim of everyone
to raise up these sparks
from wherever they are imprisoned,
and to elevate them
to holiness
by the power of their soul.

LISTENING

for Marty Ehrlich

In the dream
I watched her
as she listened to Coltrane—
eyes closed,
lips parted, descending
into the music
and further,
into the one creating it.

There was a moment
when they took a breath
together,
even though he was no longer
breathing.

CONFESSION

Words you utter out of your sleep
are food and drink for the wild angels.
—Yehuda Amichai

for Rabbi Nachman

While you were sleeping,
I saw your lips moving,
so I bent over
to hear what you were saying.
I was astonished to discover
you were telling tales in your sleep.

I was captured by those tales,
lost myself in them,
searched for myself,
repeated them
so many times,
I learned them by heart.

All it takes are the first words
of your first story
for me to find you
under an ancient oak,
next to a river of living waters,
telling your tales.

DREAMS ABOUT REB ZALMAN

1. A Visit to Reb Zalman

I'm living in another city,
in another house.
You also live there,
along with many others.
We have become very close.

Reb Zalman lives across the street.
I take you there.
When we enter,
everyone's celebrating the birth of his child,
upstairs.
There's a prayer service about to begin.
We sit together
at the back of the room.

We leave Reb Zalman's house
at dusk.
I carry you
as one might carry a child.

There's an old man
sitting on a chair outside my house,
holding a long, thin pole in his hand.
He raises it as we approach,
warning me
I'm not welcome with you.

An angel
with a flaming sword
guards the way to the tree of life.
I turn away

from the old man
and find my own path.

When I wake
a powerful longing radiates inside me.
I can still feel it
as I write this down.

2. Reb Zalman's Room

I travel to another city to visit Reb Zalman.
When I arrive at his house,
I'm led to his room.
He's standing in one corner,
playing violin,
and there are others I can't see.
When he sees me, he greets me
with a big hug,
a deep, loving one,
with nothing held back.

3. A Strange Marriage

I go down to the beach
and watch the waves,
relieved to live near the ocean at last.
After that
I meet with Reb Zalman
at his home.
There he performs a wedding for me,
although there isn't a bride.
At first I'm confused,
but then I realize he's marrying me
to myself.

TASHLIKH

You will cast all their sins into the depths of the sea.
—Micah 7:19

I reach in my pockets and pull out my sins
and cast them into the water,
sins of drought—
all the days that passed
without taking stock of my life,
sins of the flood—
when I lost my balance
and surrendered to the relentless currents.

I repent
losing the keys of faith and belief,
being silent when I should speak,
speaking when I should be silent,
destroying countless dream worlds
at the instant of waking,
ignoring the moment between ripe
and rotten.

My pockets are empty,
my sins against myself
disappearing downstream.
But I keep finding others in dark corners,
in the back of the closet,
under the sheets,
along with the bodies of all the angels
I've abandoned.

I SURRENDER

I surrender to the years.
I surrender like a vessel being emptied,
a lamp sputtering out.
I surrender my fear of extinction.
I surrender like a sunstain growing faint.

I surrender my passport.
I have no further need for it.
I surrender my travels, few that there were.
I surrender our history together to the past.
I surrender the past.

I surrender my fantasies.
I surrender to the absence of desire.
I surrender my thirst to the rain,
my breath to the wind.

HER SILENCE

in memory of Marilyn Probe

She was asleep when I arrived.
They woke her gently,
raised her bed.
She was lying back, looking very peaceful,
more beautiful than ever.

I spoke first, followed by
her silence. Yes, she listened
carefully, and sometimes shook her head,
but she could not speak.
I weighed the silence, knew
I must supply both sides
of the conversation.
So I did.

Even though she is here
she has been exiled
to a bleak land
where words are compelled to remain
unspoken.

One by one
we lose touch with each other
as we descend into the dark, floating
like feathers into the valley,
waiting to be gathered.

FIRST THE BEES

First the bees disappeared,
then the blossoms.
No one knew why.
Only the wind remained
to scatter pollen.

One dry harvest followed another.
Before long
clouds of dust traveled like pilgrims
around the planet,
searching for rain.

The seas grew dry.
The winds disappeared.
Before long
there was no one left to count
the stars.

SCENARIO

All action takes place
in the past
or future,
never in the present.
No one speaks of it.

Exploring the past,
inventing the future,
we escape
the inescapable—

until,
through no choice of our own,
we arrive at the place
where the past becomes a wall
to worship,
and the future
turns its back.

BEFORE AND AFTER

for David Meltzer

We are told not to ask what came before
or what will come after, not to ask
what is above
or what is below.
Otherwise
it would have been better
not to have been born.

Still,
we seek forbidden fruit,
climbing heavenly ladders to the stars
or diving into the deep,
searching for meaning
despite the danger
of looking back.

Those from before
left messages for us
on stone, parchment,
papyrus and clay tablets;
in journals and books,
and scrawled on napkins.
They are waiting for our reply.

Those unborn
have been silent so far.
They don't yet know
we're leaving them a world
so damaged
we're ready to abandon it
and search
for another.

JUNG'S DREAM

Traveling together on a ship,
Freud and Jung told each other their dreams.
In Jung's dream,
he was living in a house of six stories.
The top floor was the present,
but when he went downstairs
he found himself
in the past.
Each floor descended another century.
The final stairway, carved out of rock,
led him to a cave—
where a round skull was waiting.

Hearing this, Freud shouted:
That skull is me!
You desire my death!
For Freud,
Oedipus was always nearby.

As for Jung,
he found his destiny in that dream—
it revealed the many levels
of the known
and unknown,
and how to map out the great cave
of the unconscious
he would soon explore.

LIE BACK

Lie back, sink into sleep.
If you find an opening,
slip inside.

There's a whole world
hidden there,
a constellation of its own.

Every night
you must create it anew
out of the breath of stars.

DREAMS ABOUT BORGES

1. The Old Writer

I call up the old writer
and ask if I can come by for a visit.
But it's late at night,
and he isn't up to company.
He's hard at work.

2. Borges in Israel

Traveling in Israel, I happen to meet Borges.
I ask if we could talk.
Though a little reluctant,
he agrees to give me two hours of his time,
showing me the way to the house where he's staying.
Before he goes inside,
he writes the address in the book he's carrying
and gives the book to me.
For the rest of the dream
I walk back and forth,
waiting to be invited in.
When I wake I feel tricked,
because the meeting has not taken place.

3. A Secret Meeting

Borges is staying in a hotel in the town where I live.
I go there and meet with him
and discover he is now very tiny, small enough
to fit in my hand. Both of us
enjoy our meeting enormously, and when I suggest
he come back to the hotel where I'm staying,
he's happy to join me.

When we arrive, I find a place for him to hide
and sneak in food for him,
and he lets me read his new story.

4. Darkness

I'm sitting outside with Borges late at night.
He says, *I wish the darkness would come to an end.*
I say, *It will, in the morning.*
He says, *That's how you understand darkness.*
For me darkness never ends.
I seek to reassure him, saying,
Didn't darkness inspire your inner vision?
Wasn't it your destiny?
He's silent, and I can't tell
if he agrees or not.

I come back to him
whenever I close my eyes.
He is there, weighing mysteries
he alone can see in the dark.
Sometimes I hear him whispering to himself.
Then I listen carefully,
for every word that reaches me
is precious.

TALE OF THE RIVER

a Sufi parable

Long ago
two glaciers melted into each other,
forming a mighty river
that spilled forth,
pouring down mountains,
winding through forests,
making valleys fertile.
But when the river tried to cross
the desert,
it could not.
Again and again
it pushed against the sands
that held it back,
but only succeeded in creating
a swamp.

At last
a voice rose up from within, saying,
You will never get across this way.
Instead, let go of yourself,
rise up,
form a cloud
and float across.
There,
on the other side,
you will pour down as rain,
reborn as a great new river.

And the river heard that voice
and listened. Even now
a cloud is sailing across the desert,
ripening with rain.

THE DANCER

She dreams she is a ballerina dancing on stage,
and, at the same time,
watches herself from the audience.
From where she sits,
she sees her leotard is yellow,
and from the stage,
sees where she is seated.
The dance ends, the audience applauds,
the usher comes down the aisle
bringing her a bouquet
of yellow roses.

The next night
she watches herself dance again,
and sees herself from the stage.
This time her leotard is red,
and the usher brings her a bouquet
of red roses.

The third night she is afraid to sleep.
She dreams again of dancing on stage,
but her seat in the audience is empty.
The dance ends,
the audience applauds,
and the usher comes down the aisle,
bearing a black bouquet.

A PHOTO OF GOMBROWICZ

Thirty years ago,
wandering the stacks,
I pulled out a huge book
in Polish
and opened it at random
to a photo of Gombrowicz.
I had just read two of his novels
and there he was, peering out at me,
so alive
he might have stepped out of the page.

I knew he was no longer living,
but what did the one in the photograph
know of this?
We stared into each other's eyes
a long time.
Finally I closed the book,
put it back,
and never opened it again.

MEMORIES OF THE ALHAMBRA

in memory of Lyle Harris

Lyle,
I can't think of you
without seeing you cradling a guitar,
playing "Memories of the Alhambra."
You could conjure lyric gems
or build hurricane ragas.
The guitar gave into you, gave you
everything. Nothing else mattered.
Little by little, you stripped away the rest,
hidden in a small town
where the only place to play was Ramada Inn.

When you put down the guitar,
you pointed out koans
and Sufi tales, and so many books and mysteries.
You were not only the first master I met,
but a father and teacher as well.
You and Judy
were like Adam and Eve to me.

You loved that Sufi proverb:
He who sleeps on the floor
will never fall out of bed.
You spent all those years practicing
how to dispense with desire,
and when the time came,
you were ready.

Tonight,
as I finished writing these words,
there were three knocks
at the window.

I shivered at the thought
it might be you,
and for a long moment I felt your presence
here,
in this room,
as if you had stopped by.

THE GOLDEN WEB

an Egyptian Myth

In those days
everyone wove the golden web
of their lives, and as we wove,
our lives seemed to pass before us,
and we saw our future clearly.

Only later did we learn
that the images passing before us
were not an illusion;
they were life itself,
passing.

FORTY YEARS LATER

for Deena

One night I fell asleep in her arms,
and when I woke up, forty years later,
she was gone.
There was no sign of her,
no hair on the pillow, no scent
of her perfume, nothing
except for a little book she had left me.
With no other clue, I read it.
The words rose up from the page
in a whisper, beckoning me
to search for her.

When I got up, I discovered I had plunged
into old age. My hair was gray, my legs stiff.
I wasn't hungry, or even thirsty,
but my heart was full of longing.
Surely she must have tried to wake me,
but my sleep was so deep,
my dreams so compelling,
she could not.
By now, I knew, she must be married,
with a family,
having left me far behind.

I soon discovered
there were no maps to find lost loves.
Still, I filled bottles with messages
and cast them into the currents,
hoping one would reach her.
But I heard nothing.
So I sent out books into the world,
books only she was certain

I would write.
Yet while I heard from many others,
she was silent.

I tell myself,
perhaps she prefers to forget,
or perhaps she wants to remember us
as we were,
or perhaps one day
her heart will open long enough
to glimpse
all we left behind.

A PALACE OF BIRD BEAKS

for Dan Jaffe

I've built a shelter
out of words
fragile as a palace
of bird beaks.

I put down
the foundation
when Adam lost
his rib.

I knew
it must last
a lifetime,
and it has.

When this shelter
came into being,
I was born.

If it remains
our secret,
so be it.

BECOMING A BOOK

When writers die they become books, which is, after all,
not too bad an incarnation."
        —Jorge Luis Borges

for Ben Furnish

All these years,
without knowing it,
I've been preparing for my rebirth
as a book.

Each day
I try to condense
light and darkness
into one more page.

At night
I count the pages left
before it's time
to come back.

Now that my destiny is known,
we need not say goodbye.
I'll be there guarding you
from a shelf.

A SANCTIFICATION CEREMONY

for Jocelyne

Asleep in your cellar,
I dream repeatedly of a ceremony
you perform for your sons,
calling on your ancestors
and the angels
to assist you.
I watch,
a skeptical witness,
as the ceremony takes place.

Afterward,
just before waking,
I see your purpose—
to sanctify
the son without
and the son within.

On waking
I feel much better,
as if I were the one
who has been sanctified.
This lasts many hours.

PASSAGE

We have dreamt the world.
—Jorge Luis Borges

We walk through streets half-foreign,
half-familiar, past houses
half-lighted, half in darkness.
When we reach your house we say goodbye.
Only later do I remember the book
I left with you, and it doesn't matter
if it was written or not,
for I know this must be a dream,
and that I'll choose
to wake up.

So I leave one world and give myself
to another, and in this way enter
a great darkness,
where no world exists.
The darkness grows vaster
and my fear increases.
There's no simple passage
from one world to the next,
and I, who created that dream world,
must now recreate the one
in which I'll wake.

Just then
something appears in the dark
close enough for me to reach for,
and as I do, I wake up,
resting on my bed,
in this room,
and it's day.

MOONTIDE

The river rises above the trees.
—I Ching

Late at night
I sat beneath a tree,
leaning against the trunk.

All at once
the moon slipped from the sky,
through the branches,
into a river
swelling from unseen roots.

While I watched,
as if no longer there,
the tide passed over the tree,
and I disappeared.

THE WHITE DEER

A small white deer with antlers
wants to come into my room,
to sleep at the foot of my bed.
This time I let him in.
Somehow he brings the forest
with him.
As long as he's here,
I sleep peacefully
beneath a canopy of stars.

ERRATA

for Judy Kerman

By necessity,
every book must have at least one flaw:
a misprint, a missing page,
one imperfection.
What would happen
if each letter should appear
exactly as intended?
As it is some books,
nearly perfect,
are known to become transparent
when opened under the proper constellation,
when the full moon rests in place.

Then it's not uncommon
to become lost in a single letter,
or to hear a voice rise up
from the silent page,
Then only one imperfect letter,
one missing page,
can permit you
to pull up the covers around you
and sleep.

II

BREATHING IN THE DARK

(2011)

BREATHING IN THE DARK

for Ava

So many months breathing in the dark—
the scent of underground springs
sustains you,
a hidden moon beckons you
to grow ripe.

While you sleep,
an angel whispers the secrets of creation,
showing you
every branch of the tree of life.
Someday
you will dimly recall
all that was revealed,
roots,
and branches,
and breath.

You wake,
a lilac
waiting for the wind,
a sensual stone,
a leaf
thirsty for a kiss.
From now on
you will wake with this thirst
every morning
and drink in
everything
until the crickets rub their wings together,
singing.

MY FATHER HAD MANY PROFESSIONS

My father had many professions,
all at the same time—
watchmaker,
jeweler,
antique dealer—
first at every estate sale.
Once in a while I went with him,
saw him bargain
and barter,
try to eke out a few bucks.

He often wished
for a shop of his own,
but when Max offered to back him,
he turned him down.
He was too restless
to stay in one place.

We never knew
what he would bring home—
old watches,
gold wedding rings,
a real working slot machine,
once, puppies
hidden in his pockets.

After dinner
he sat down at the dining-room table,
put on his jeweler's loupe,
and studied every item,
reciting its history for my mother and sister,
who sat with him for hours,
while I lay in bed upstairs,
reading.

A LETTER TO MY UNCLE HOWARD

in memory of Howard Rubin

One day,
during the war,
while working at Wabash Station,
something exploded inside my mother
and she broke down, crying.
Three days later
she learned
of your death that day,
when your ship was bombed.
You were twenty-eight.

You had a hard life.
Your mother, Sarah,
died giving birth to you.
Your desperate father sought out a bride
and was set up with Rose,
my grandmother.
They had four of their own.
Rose never liked you.
You were said to resemble your mother.

Your left arm,
broken in childhood,
never grew again.
You hide it in the few photos I have of you.
Still, you were a world traveler,
standing before the Parthenon
in one photo
and somewhere in the East
in another.

Uncle, we never met,

but my mother often told me
how much she loved you,
her older brother.
She named me after you.
You taught me a great lesson.
Because of you
I decided never to go to war.
You had already lost your life.
That was enough.

INHERITANCE

My mother and father
each left me
a single story.

When I was a child
my mother told me about the angel Lailah,
who whispered stories to me
before I was born.
But as soon as I took a breath,
Lailah put her finger to my lips
as a reminder
to keep those stories
secret.

When I was older
my father told me
about all the demon children
a man fathers in his lifetime
with Lilith, queen of demons,
and how, on his deathbed,
all his unborn children flock around him,
crying out his name.

This, then, is my inheritance:
from my mother,
a mark on my lips
where I was sworn to silence;
from my father,
invisible offspring
calling out my name.

NEW SKIN

for Nati

My son
tells me
he has shed his American skin,
burned it
and buried it.
So too has he abandoned
his mother tongue
for his mother's tongue—
now he speaks,
thinks,
even dreams
in Hebrew,
and only speaks English
to me.

A photo arrives
of a young soldier
dressed in olive green,
married to his gun.
Only his smile is familiar.
We battle at a great distance
over his safety.
All the other fathers
take pride
in the young warriors they bequeath
to their nation.
His father
doesn't like armies
at all.

OARS

The boat's a beauty—
simple,
spare,
carved out of a single trunk,
agile enough
to steer through rapids
or high waves.

Before he set out
we said, *Wait!*
Be sure to stock up
on supplies.
Don't forget a fishing pole.
Above all,
don't leave your oars behind.

But the sea shone so brightly,
the sands were so enticing,
the water so blue,
the waves so alluring
and the wind—
the wind was so young
and vital.

A PORTRAIT OF MY SON

for Nati

He has climbed high in the branches of almond trees
to shake them free of their fruit,
harvested holy weed,
braided challahs while it was still dark,
hawked warm loaves in the *shuk*,
worked on a dig by the Wall.

He is full of contradictions:
a sniper with a conscience,
an impatient student who loves to read,
a would-be chef, tour guide, translator.
When here, he longs to be there;
when there, he longs to be here.

He ignores the wisdom of the Fathers
and the wisdom of his father,
preferring the mystery of being
with no questions asked.
What he loves
is to feel the wind in his face,
and to bask in the warmth of the sun.

SPIRIT GUIDE

for Miriam

One morning
Miriam woke up
holding her grandmother's hand.
Savta had come to her
from the spirit world
to reveal
that the souls of her children
have already chosen her,
and that in a past life
she and Savta
were sisters.

Savta tells
of traveling
with many spirit beings,
of being busy with old souls,
and with helping children
cross over.
She has brought Miriam three gifts
that need to be revealed:
a gold bracelet,
a blue shawl for protection,
and a white lily
for her heart.

Kissing her forehead,
touching her hair,
Savta stays close by.
*You're here
and I'm here,* she whispers,
but I will always be with you.
Among the secrets she reveals:
journey like a river,
sing like a sweet bird,
let the angels in.

AFTERLIFE

It was very hard for me to descend to you.
—Rabbi Nachman

Before this page grows blank
let me send you this message
from the afterlife.
I've written it in letters
that will fade
at the first light.
Still, just the heat of your hand
would be enough
to burn these letters into being.

Whether you know it or not,
you have called me forth.
I have come a long way to bring you
strength,
faith,
and wisdom.

Whenever you want me,
plant a seed
in the darkest place,
tend it in secret,
and it will bring forth
a tree of blessings.

ARI IN THE FOREST

Child
of my child,
I take you for a walk in the forest.
Your hand in mine,
I feel like a creator
as I reveal this world
of shadows and light
to you.

Nothing in your experience
of rooms and parks
has prepared you
for this unbounded place.
But you take it all in stride,
following the forest path
wherever it goes.

Resting on a log,
you peer into the branches,
seeing the world with the new eyes
I long for.
I, like you,
came here
from a place of darkness
and made it my home.

AVA

All of us enwrapped,
growing together,
rooted like a tree at the river's edge,
leaning toward the waters,
casting our own shadow,
complete
in ourselves

My father once said,
I am the trunk,
you are the branches.
Now, from the top branch,
a baby tumbles into my arms,
her body pale,
her eyes closed.

Somehow
I caught her,
saved her
from the current.
And now as I hold her
I start to chant,
Don't let the baby die!

Who will welcome her?
After all,
we are already complete.
But I keep chanting until,
at the end of the dream,
Ava opens her eyes.

RETIREMENT

In the dream I came back to my office.
It was empty,
except for a bird I had left behind.
It had been many months,
but the bird still perched above the door.
Light was pouring in,
and the room was calm,
and I thought it would be a good place
to write.

While the door was open,
the bird flew out.
But I didn't mind.
I knew someone else
would feed her.

DREAM VISIT

for Maury Schwartz

My uncle Maury,
now in his eighties,
comes to visit me in a dream.
He's in his late twenties
and quite tall.
He calmly takes a seat
in my hotel room.
I'm still in bed.

We chat in the dark.
He says,
I think I need to go to the hospital.
I say, *I'll take you.*
He says, *No, it's better if you call.*

Who can forget
how he drove to the hospital
with his father collapsed on his shoulder,
no longer breathing?

Once,
soon after my father died,
I dreamed that my uncle was condemned
to be hung. After that
it would be my turn.

Now we are silent.
His calm radiates throughout the room.
I'm not sure if it's morning or not—
the curtain next to him
is closed.

SIGNS OF THE LOST TRIBE

for Rodger Kamenetz

One day
I found the first sign:
old boxes stacked in the attic
in a room I had never entered.
After that
I found signs everywhere:
in every drawer I opened,
on every doorpost I passed,
when I lay down
and when I rose up.

Somehow
one of the ten lost tribes
had wandered out of the desert,
and all of them were living
in my house.

Since then
I have become accustomed
to their ways.
Of course, I never acknowledge
their presence.
Who knows
what they would do
if their secret were known?

They have traveled in exile
ever since they were born,
following the path of the exodus
wherever it leads them.
They still fulfill the rituals
carved out of so many years

of wandering:
blessing the moon,
counting the stars,
casting their sins in the water.

During the day
they search everywhere
for the land that has been lost.
At night, they hide
from the unsuspecting
in closets filled with invisible families,
in drawers crowded with sorrows,
on shelves full of their sad
songs.

They even inhabit
my dreams.
There,
above all,
they are at home.

A WALL RUBBING

for Yitzhak Greenfield

Late at night,
when no one else was nearby,
we reached the Wall.
There, while you stood guard,
I held this page against a stone
and began to rub.

Soon, dark letters began to emerge
that slowly formed themselves
into words.
I tried to decipher them,
but there was not enough light.

When the rubbing was finished,
we hurried home
to read what was written there.
But the words,
like tears,
were mute,
and all we could discover
in the imprint of that ancient stone
was a long silence.

THE TOMB OF THE ARI

for Jocelyne and Shimon Elbaz

We descend
into the steep valley of bones,
accompanied by a white butterfly
fluttering in and out of sight,
leading us on.
Footsteps of past centuries
rush by in the wind.
The dust remembers
your presence
in this place.

At last I place my hand
on your tomb,
painted blue.
As I do, you ask me
what I want,
and my reply rises up
on its own:
to be a vessel.

Later, we ascend to your ritual bath
in a cave
fed by a cool stream.
Each time I submerge
I feel danger and blessing
bound together in a single breath.
I immerse myself three times,
cleansed of regret.

SONGS OF NAZINE

Summoned or not, the gods will come.
—C. G. Jung

1. Her Creation

No sooner have I named her,
than she begins to speak.
Fire is always her first word,
then *water*.
Out of these
worlds can be created.

2. Her Thirst

With each step she takes
a restless sea of sand
erases her footprints.

Still
her thirst has brought her this far.
She is not about
to turn back.

2. Her Descent

She never forgets
her descent,
not during the plague of locusts,
not during the plague
of darkness.

During the day,
she counts the sands of the shore.
At night, she counts the stars.

3. Her Faith

At first she swore to be satisfied
with one God,
then she discovered two.

At first she believed her name
would be carved in stone.
Later she tasted the waters of oblivion.

4. A Single Candle

Night lasts so long.
Even the stars
rise and set
in secret.

Once she knew
how to use darkness
and death
to bring forth light.

When there is only
a single candle left,
she closes her eyes
and tries to remember
the sun.

5. In the Dark

Tonight
Nazine and I
sit facing each other
in the dark.
She is barefoot
and I secretly caress
her feet.

SIGNS

One after another,
they come into your life pointing the way—
a rain of blessings or curses
floating down from the sky like feathers,
burning in fire like tortoise shells,
swirling at the bottom of the cup.

They fall
like manna at your feet.
Every dream is littered with them,
every bird's song contains a strong hint,
every oracle
spells out your fate.

With so many warnings
how can you go wrong?
There's the rub—
before you can follow the signs,
you must be able to read them.

TRIBE OF THE JEWELERS

While others see a landscape
of rocks and sand
stretching before them,
they perceive the jewel
concealed in every rock
like a hidden sun.
In their hands
the layers of the past peel away
like the skin of an orange,
revealing the precious core
within.

The secrets of the jewelers
are passed down
from father to son:
how to distinguish what is precious
from what is not;
how to cut away what is not needed;
how to set free
all the hidden facets.

This is my tribe.
I can still see my father
bent over a table,
peering into the eye of the jewel.
Even now,
as I bend over this page,
I can hear him whispering
my name.

THREE POEMS ABOUT THE MOON

1. The Face of the Moon

Last night,
when the face of the moon
was hidden,
I leaned closer
to catch her whispered words,
but she was gone.

2. The Moon I Carved

The moon I carved out of my dreams
is missing.

What night does it illumine now?

If I cross to the other side
will I find it there?

The moon I carved out of my dreams
is missing.

Where should I look for it
now?

3. Bearing the Moon

Slowly
the new moon gives way
to one I can hold.

I see a flock of sparrows
bearing the moon

on their wings.
They leave me this message:

Wherever you wander,
take the moon with you.

FOREPLAY

My words caress your ear
like little bird tongues,
exploring secret passages and hidden chambers,
beckoning sighs,
arousing suppressed desires,
reading between the lines.

Eyes closed,
you weigh every word,
letting its meaning sink in
and take root.
Before long
something begins to stir:
a seed,
a bud,
a living breath.

WAKING TOO LATE

How many winters
did I sleep
without waking,
the image of the moon
fading in my eyes?

You woke me
with gentle, insistent questions.
There was something in your voice
that recalled
the rain
falling through branches,
the sound of the wind in the leaves,
the way a tree breathes
in the dark.
Little by little
the world took form
and we were the only
inhabitants.

At first that world seemed boundless.
Later, it shrank
to the size of a root.
For this was not the same world
I had left behind,
but another,
far crueler,
where even the rising of the moon
was just a rehearsal,
and we were only ghosts
who had never lived.

DESCENT

You are sad tonight.
I would go to you
but your door is shut to everyone,
even yourself.

I imagine you
descending the stairs
to your cellar,
where even a flashlight
can't illuminate the dark.

I imagine you
sinking into shadowy waters,
and I want to rescue you,
but I can't reach you.

If I could just hold you
and whisper to you
and reassure you
and calm you
and let you rest
and let you find your trust again
and find the love
that keeps getting lost—

but the door is shut
to everyone,
even yourself.

A BROKEN THREAD

All that remained
was a broken
thread.

Still
I clung to it,
determined to weave
a blanket
of stars,

a coat for the moon
we could wear
together.

LAMENT

Today as it grew dark
I recalled how once after leaving you
I vowed
to take care,
so there would never be a night
when I would walk outside
and realize
I had lost your love.

That was many years ago,
yesterday.
Still, a voice within
keeps repeating
your name.

No, you are not here.
Only in rare dreams are we together
for a long, intimate moment.

I know—
the faces of our children
bear the imprint
of our branching paths—

there's no turning back
to before they were born.

DREAM CHILD

for Melissa Gurley Bancks

A dream child
has come a great distance
to bring you a gift—
an ornate silver box,
rare and precious.

She opens the box
and calls for you to come closer.
Like a sleepwalker you obey.
Inside, you see
a handful of black petals
fashioned from onyx,
a bouquet
of black fire.

Even now
she is holding out this gift for you,
waiting for you to take it—
to bring back those dark petals,
those poems
begging to be born,
those secrets only a dream child
could understand.

SWIMMING TO JERUSALEM

The first time
I went on a quest
for forbidden fruit.

The second time
I built an ark
and tried to get there by sea.

The third time
I came in search of my ancestor,
Abraham.

If the sun was hidden,
I let the stars
guide me.

If the tablets were broken,
I carved
new ones.

In the future
my bones
will roll to that city.

Last night
I dreamed
I was swimming there.

THE HIDDEN LIGHT

God said, Let there be light,
and there was light.
—Genesis 1:3

In the light of the first day
it was possible to see
to the ends of the universe.

What happened to that light?
Some say it can be found in Paradise,
as a reward for the souls
of the righteous.
Others say
it's hidden in the stories of the Torah,
and whenever those stories are told,
a ray of this light
comes forth.

I say
there's a ray of that light hidden
in every page,
even this one,
waiting to be set free.

THE FIRST EVE

Male and female He created them.
—Genesis 1:27

As Adam watched,
the first Eve was created
from the inside out—
first her bones,
then her flesh,
finally she was covered
with skin.
But when God offered her to Adam,
he fled in disgust.

So the first Eve
was taken away,
never to be heard from again.
And Adam was put to sleep.
And when he awoke
there was another woman,
one created from his own rib,
a woman close to his heart.

But what of the first Eve?
No one knows her fate—
whether she was taken into paradise
or uncreated.

Even now
she haunts us from the shadows,
calling Adam's name.

LILITH'S CAVE

Lilith turns away
from the eye that is always open,
from the hand that holds her back.
Fettered by the ancient vow,
she crawls back
into her cave,
coiled inside the roots
of dreams.

Every night I fall asleep in that cave.
As soon as I close my eyes, I sink
into her embrace.
Her breath rises and falls, her arms
pull me closer,
until I'm inside her
and she's inside
me.

Too late, I invoke the names of angels—
only dark spirits come forth,
flocking around me,
crying out her name.
Before long
she has taken everything,
sacred or profane,
and given me nothing
in return.

CAIN

The old man has been stopped
trying to cross the border.
His passport has been taken away,
and three witnesses are preparing
to testify against him.

But the old man understands
nothing of this.
His crime, if any,
has grown vague to him in time.
His victim, a brother or son,
perhaps the only man ever to employ him…
these are facts he has forgotten.

The sign on his forehead,
to signify and protect him in his wanderings,
has worn away.
He no longer remembers what it was.
For him, the circle has grown tighter
than a knot:
he is always standing at the border,
he is always stopped,
his passport always taken.

Each time
the same witnesses denounce him
with the same testimony,
but he never refutes their words,
or even listens to what they say.

And each time his passport is handed back,
the curse and warning
are spelled out
in a writing he can't read,
in a language he can't comprehend.

RIVER DREAM

In the dream
I'm on one side of a river,
and there is a woman bathing a baby
in the cool water on the other side.
As evening falls,
she places the baby in a basket
and sets it afloat
to me.

Even though she can't see me,
she knows I'm here,
waiting for the basket to arrive.
Nor can I see her,
but I know she has set it
adrift.

OUT OF EGYPT

At first
I was your master,
you, my slave.
But we traded places,
and I've been your slave
ever since.

You taunt
and tantalize me,
command me to come closer,
then cast me out.
How long
will I have to mourn in the desert
this time?

At night
the locusts insist
it's time to take leave of you,
to abandon your embrace.
But I have been a slave so long
I cannot bear
to go.

THE FIERY SERPENTS

And the Lord sent fiery serpents among the people,
and they bit the people.
—Numbers 21:6

These serpents
consist entirely of fire.
They leap out of the flames
and bite you as you sleep,
causing nightmares so terrible
you wake up
grateful
to be breathing.

This happens
night after night
until, in your desperation,
you put out the fire.
And still the fiery serpents crawl out of the ashes
like long-lost embers,
and the nightmares they bring
are the worst of all.

THE ANGEL OF LOSSES

after Rabbi Nachman of Bratslav

for Rabbi Marc Soloway

There is an angel
who watches over us,
even in the dark.
He watches lives unfold,
recording every detail
before it fades.
This angel carries a shovel,
and spends his time digging,
searching for losses.
For a great deal has been lost.

He knows it's necessary
to search in the dark,
not with a torch,
but with a small candle.
That's all you need
to search inside wells,
where darkness is unbroken,
peering into every corner.

It's enough
to be guided by that light,
small though it may be.

TWO MEDITATIONS

1. Guide

for Michael Castro

With eyes closed,
peer into the dark
and try to read the letters written
behind your eyelids.
Those letters spell out a word,
a holy name—
the name of the angel
who guides you.
Pronounce it silently to yourself.

Now,
keeping that name in mind,
let the letters rearrange themselves
until they spell out
another word.
That is your secret name,
the name with which your mother blessed you
when you took your first breath.

She carried it with her
all those months
in your long journey from darkness.
It bears
all her hopes and blessings for you,
spoken and unspoken,
in this world
and the next.

2. Hidden Gate

for Rabbis Susan Talve and Jim Goodman

Focus
on one letter
at a time.
Stare at it
until nothing else exists.

Now that you and the letter
are one,
search for its hidden gate.
If you can find it,
you may glimpse a burning bush,
hear a voice out of a whirlwind,
or follow a path through the sea.

These visions have been passed down
by those who came before us.
Our task
is to weave them
into a single story
that will descend a heavenly ladder
to reach us.

A VISION

for Dennis Crowe

Forty years ago,
late at night,
you hurled a question at me
and triggered a vision—
my soul took leave of my body,
and I saw myself from a great distance
as a tree on fire,
shivering in fear.

For a long moment I hovered on high,
rooted in the eternal,
then I found myself
back in my body,
convulsed with weeping.

FEATHERS

for Ruth Krasnoff

Before she died,
your mother promised to visit you.
Whenever she did,
she would leave a feather behind.
Ever since, you have encountered,
in the most unlikely places,
a solitary feather.

If you pick up that feather
you might hear her whisper—
Listen, if you only knew
how easy it is
to glide away from this world,
all your fear
would vanish.

Surely those feathers
fell through the cracks
between worlds,
to remind you
how much is hidden.

EXPLORING THE DARK

for Charles Simic

First you must forget everything,
even the alphabet.
Whatever you discover there
must be
for the first time.

When you are ready,
lower yourself
into a well,
make your way
through underground caverns,
or descend the stairway into darkness.

It would be easy to become lost down there,
but there's no need for that—
you have almost reached the shore
of the dark sea,
where a boat is waiting.

THE STORY

for Steve Stern

The story
burrowed into the cellar
till it reached roots.
It suckled those roots
and decided not to stop there.
It burrowed
into the past,
where the whispering of the dead
is incessant.

At first, all the story could catch
were a few scattered words,
but before long
the words insisted
the story link them together.
So it did.

Now the past
wants that story back.
But the story insists
it belongs to them
both.

DREAMS ABOUT KAFKA

1. Arrival

God, in the form of a large, strong man
with the kind face
of Franz Kafka,
picks me up from behind
and brings me into this world,
whispering in my ear.

2. A Gathering

Many famous writers have gathered in my living room.
One by one, I lead them out of the house.
A few are reluctant to go.
Finally only Kafka and Borges remain,
and I let them stay.

3. A Kafka Festival

A Kafka festival is being held in my town.
I'm told of an official
who can put me in touch with Kafka's family.
The official turns out to be a skeleton
with hollow, empty eyes.
He resists strenuously—
striking my arm three times
with his bony arm—
but finally gives up the number.
Just as I place the call,
somebody disconnects me,
insisting my time is up.

4. Kafka Came Back

Kafka came back—
he was reborn
or came alive again.
He wrote new stories
that he let me read.
We were friends.
I shared his new stories with you.

5. Kafka's Hidden Garden

There's a hidden garden in Kafka's writings,
always implied,
never stated,
a hidden place of release.
The quotes supporting it
are slender but enticing,
as if it were a great secret.

6. Departure

God—
or is it Kafka?—
tells me it's time to go,
puts his arms around me from behind,
picks me up gently
and takes me away from this world,
whispering in my ear.

CITY OF THE DEAD

in memory of Rabbi Arnold Asher

The road I took
in that city
was round.

It was said
that all who started out on that road
would one day meet
all the others
who followed its path.

I was searching for you.
At the same time
I was afraid
I would find you.

KADDISH ON A BRIDGE

In Memory of Leon Hereid

Your young daughter Hannah
says she saw you that night
floating on the ceiling of her room.
When you descended
she gave you a cookie,
you gave her a kiss.

In one photo,
surrounded by your family,
you peer at us
from the beyond, asking,
How could this have happened to me?

Leon, the last time I saw you
was at your wedding.
Now we are saying kaddish.
Here, on this bridge
where your ashes were scattered,
we count our blessings
and number our days.

THE LIBRARY OF DREAMS

Gathered in that library
are the collected dreams
of all the great dreamers,
known
and unknown.

From his place among the immortals,
Borges visits this library every night.
Standing before its shelves,
he can perceive all those dreams at once,
as if in the Aleph.
If only he could send the most memorable
out into the world
like seeds.
But the dream librarian has sworn him
to silence.

An opium dream transported Coleridge
to this library, where he read a poem
about an emperor's palace.
Once awake, he began to write it down,
but before he could finish,
the librarian arrived,
disguised as a man from Porlock.

Even you have found your way
to the library of dreams
only to discover
that all the pages of its books are blurred
unless you bring them, line by line,
into being.
But by then the librarian is beside you,
closing the book,
putting it back on the shelf.

And by the time you realize
that the words you read there
were your own,
it's too late.

A JOURNEY TO THE LAND OF THE SUN

It's a tale so long
all you can remember
is the ending—
arriving in that fabled land,
culmination
of a long quest.

Everything else about it
has been lost.

THE WINE CELLAR

I was confined with my father
in a small room,
a wine cellar.
He was trying to sleep.
I could barely see in the dark.
It was becoming harder
and harder
to breathe.
Just as the iron door
was about to shut,
I forced my way out.

I woke in the dark,
relieved,
sat up and breathed in
and out,
grateful to be breathing.

CONTEMPLATING MY OWN SKELETON

a shamanistic exercise

I remember the sun
till no voice remains
to call the moon closer.

I remember the moon
till no waves remain
to wash over sandstone.

I remember the waves
till no wind remains
to scatter my ashes.

I remember the wind
till no sand remains
to cover my bones.

I remember
my bones.

IN THAT COUNTRY

You will find no other lands.
—C. P. Cavafy

In that country
there are no gates
to enter or exit.
No passports are required.
No visas to be stamped.
By the time you get there
it's already too late
to turn back.

In that country
there is no waiting for rooms,
nor any rooms for waiting.
Despite all your plans,
no one comes to welcome you.
The phones are all silent.
The traffic has come to a halt.

There are no maps to read,
no landmarks to guide you,
no signposts,
no stations on the way.
Besides, all the roads
lead to the same place.

In that country
all the histories remain unwritten,
all the books are blank.
Not even the cycle of the seasons
is known,
or how long you must stay
before you can set out
for somewhere else.

SINGING BONES

Can these bones live?
—Ezekiel 37:3

for Jerred Metz

The time had come
for the bones to rise up
but there was no breath in them.

If only they could find shelter
under the tree of life,
this time
they would turn away
from the tree of death.

If only a young shepherd
would carve a flute out of one of them
and play it,
that singing bone would speak
of all that remains
unspoken.

They listen breathlessly
for the word that will attach
tendons to flesh
and cover them with skin.
At any moment, surely,
it will be spoken.

MISSISSIPPI JOHN HURT BURIED
IN THE PEPPER

The sky broke open
and it was raining pepper.
Pepper was falling all around him.
It was pouring pepper.
The pepper was coming home to roost.

The pepper was black and white—
who would ever know it?
Clouds of pepper—
who had ever seen it?
John Hurt held up his umbrella
but it was filled with pepper.

The earth had fallen into
a pepper pot.
Clouds of pepper hid the sun.
Clouds of pepper hid the clouds.
The fine earth was filled
with pepper dust.

John Hurt was a root
buried in the pepper.
John Hurt felt the long arm of the pepper.
John Hurt felt the pepper rise up
around his neck.

It was time to go.
It sure was a lot of pepper.

A VISION

for Jules Steimnitz

That summer
we went to one of the islands,
expecting shores of pristine sand.
Instead, the beach outside our window
was covered with ashes.

For twelve days
we lived with those ashes.
Then, on the last night,
just before I went to sleep,
the wall on the other side of the room
vanished, and I saw a beach—

not the same beach
we had walked on—
but a beach of the whitest sands,
surrounded by a golden aura.
For a long moment I stared at it,
but I grew afraid
and turned on the light
and that unblemished beach
disappeared

and I found myself back in a room
facing the sea,
where none of the walls
were missing.

THE LAST SUNSET

in memory of Gabriel Preil

Surely Gabriel knew
he might be returning to Jerusalem
to take his leave
of this world.
But how could he have known
it would come
on a Friday night,
in the arms of the Sabbath Queen?

The collector of autumns and sunsets
has himself been gathered
in the holy land,
in the city
where his soul resided
even when his body
was far away.

If only he could tell us
what that last sunset
was like.

YEHUDA AMICHAI
IN THE HEAVENLY JERUSALEM

On earth,
in his beloved Jerusalem,
he could often be found in that tiny café
on King George,
sipping black coffee.
Everyone knew who he was,
but they all left him alone.
Later, he would shop in the *shuk*
like everyone else,
take a seat in the back of the bus,
put down his bags of fruits and vegetables,
and dream a little
till the bus reached his stop.

Everyone else was asleep
when he rose at four in the morning
to jot down the poems hidden in the corners
of his city.
This was his secret life.

On his seventieth birthday he whispered,
I'm tired of giving birth,
and it seemed to be true.
His face was tired,
even his eyes,
and yet something continued to burn.

I've learned the secret
of fertilizing myself, he told me.
I supply both egg and seed.
But I'm tired of giving birth.

At seventy-six
he took leave of this world
quietly,
as one would expect of such a modest man.
Presidents and prime ministers spoke at his funeral;
thousands gathered to pay their respects.
When he reached heaven,
he was greeted by his heroes,
King David and Shmuel ha-Nagid,
along with hundreds of his poems,
their flying letters swirling around him.
The angels, delighted to welcome him,
offered him a pair of wings,
but he declined, saying,
It's enough if my words have wings.
Tell me, where are the cafés?

Other souls
wander the streets of Paradise like tourists,
staring at the heavenly temple
or taking a seat at the back of Rashi's class.
Not Yehuda.
He's still longing for the ruins
of the earthly temple,
for the ancient stones of his earthly city,
for all the sheets hung out to dry,
flapping like sails in the wind.

A SHELTER OF STARS

The whole universe is the Temple of God.
—Philo

We live
in a shelter of stars,
our breath
one of many winds
set free in this place.

We live
in a shelter of branches,
the roof a firmament of stars,
the cellar
a dark sea.

We live
in a shelter of song,
a tabernacle of peace,
our breath as fragile and wild
as any wind.

III

SLEEPWALKING BENEATH THE STARS

(1992)

SLEEPWALKING BENEATH THE STARS

She seems to float
no higher than a hand's breadth
across the field.
Somehow
she knows exactly where she is going,
as if her palm were a map of the orchard
she has entered,
a braille landscape waiting to be read.

By now you know
how dangerous it would be
to wake her—
the star
that rises and sets in the branches
would begin to fade,
the names of the leaves would be lost.
Still,
even the slightest wind
threatens to carry her off,
her frail image almost lost in the darkness
as she passes between
two trees.

Even now
frightened stars hide their light
and every blossom holds its breath,
for if the plague of darkness lasts much longer,
she too may be enslaved by silence
and never emerge from the orchard
in peace.

MIRIAM'S WELL

Every place our forefathers went,
the well went before them.
—Pirke de Rabbi Eliezer

Her well
wanders with me,
even when I am lost.

Yet it's always
nearby,
like a golden dove
buried beneath
the sand.

If only I could hold it in my hands,
surely
the heat would warm
its wings,
surely
it would take
flight—

If only
I could remember
my thirst,
I would know where to look for it
with my eyes
closed.

THE SCRIBE

Even now
he is watching your life unfold,
recording every detail
before it fades,
before the dark side takes root,
before the roots descend
to the cave
of the forgotten
sea.

Later
he will sift through everything,
casting days
and years
into a black hole,
saving only a kernel
ripe enough
to remember.

MERMAIDS

They are Pharaoh's children
drowned
in the Red Sea,
old women
banished
from the face of the earth.

They are spirits of the deep
called forth,
daughters of the sea
and sun,
a race of dolphins
who mated with men.

Their sisters, the sirens,
cry out to the waves,
embracing them,
gathering the souls
of the drowned
into their domain.

One of them always turns up
when you drift in the Lost Sea—
which one
will it be
this time?

GOING BACK

All night
the shadow of an ancient bird
circled around me,
each turning taking me back
one year
at a time.

Back
until it was time to be
reborn,
back even further,
until all I could remember
was how a seed
grows ripe.

Back
to the instant
I was conceived,
peering out the door
of the seed
at spinning planets of light
rising up
from below.

Still
the ancient bird
circled,
but I knew
if I went back
any further,
I might not be able
to return.

THE COVENANT OF THE STARS

Look now toward heaven and count the stars,
if you are able to. So shall be thy seed.

—Genesis 15:5

I tried
to escape
the covenant of the sands,
every demand
of destiny,
every shadow
of the law.
I hid
from the pillar of salt
by day,
ran from the pillar of fire
at night.

Still
the covenant of the stars
beckoned,
each star
a rain of blessings,
a seed taking root,
a tent of meeting
between I
and thou.

THE DARK ORCHARD

Four sages entered an orchard.
—The Talmud

Better to sail on an unknown sea
than to become lost
in that garden
of forking
paths.

One
who entered
looked and died,
one looked
and lost his mind,
one cut the shoots,
cutting himself off.
Only one
entered and departed
in peace.

Those who wander there
know there is no exit,
only a caravan
of spirits,
all those who have gone before us
in search
of light.

DREAM PALM

The right has memorized
ancient histories,
entrances and exits,
angles of repose
and abandoned maps.
Someday its lifeline will serve
as a deathmask.

But the left—
all its coastlines are uncharted,
its deserts undiscovered,
its clay incomplete,
an eyeless needle
sworn to silence.

THE RAG AND BONE SHOP

The finest clothes turn to rags.
—I Ching

Perhaps
you are looking for it
in the wrong place—
no, it's not in the cellar,
behind a locked door.

It's not in a dark cave.
Not in a dry well.
Not in a field or forest.
Not in an orchard or garden.
Not in a blessing,
not in a curse.
Not on the first day,
not on the last.

Not in the feast,
not in the famine,
not in the planting,
not in the growing ripe.
Not in all you can remember,
not in all you would
forget.

Not in the stars.
Not in the graves.
Not in the rags.
Not in the bones.
Not here.
Not yet.

THE PIT OF BABEL

In your wanderings
you may have stumbled
on the Pit of Babel,
the mouth
of the abyss,
the fault line
always ready
to crack.

Even now
you may be standing
on it.

SALT

in memory of Harry Weber

Salt
became so scarce
it was worth its weight in gold.
Not only the shelves
were empty—
the salt
had even vanished
from the sea.

What little
was left
we hoarded.
Too soon
even the hoards
were empty.

We dug in the earth
everywhere,
searching for salt.
But it had all
disappeared.

Salt was more precious
than the veins in which
it flowed.
They were willing to kill
for it.

I have a little salt left.
I'm afraid
they will try to take it
away.

COURTING OBLIVION

Come here,
she says,
dancing on the edge,
flicking one rose petal
after another
into the abyss.

And every hour
you move one step closer,
your eyes fixed
on the breast
that has almost torn free
from her gown,
averted from the other,
dry as a raisin,
from which she suckles
death.

But which one will she offer?

Come here
she whispers,
crooking her finger,
swaying her hips,
come closer.

THE CAVE OF THE FOUR WINDS

The cave of the four winds
is covered by a curtain.
If only a corner of that curtain
is lifted,
the winds
will bring down a gentle rain
of blessings.

But if the curtain is pulled apart,
the covenant of being
will be broken—

breath will be torn
from every body,
the world will return
to chaos.

In the cave
behind the curtain
even the winds
hold their breath.

ORACLE OF THE OIL

for Laura Fishman

When every shadow and every echo
have disappeared,
pour a little oil
into the hollow of your hand,
enough to form a small mirror.

Soon
worlds will come into being
and disappear,
a sea of stars
taking root in your hand.

Look closely
before the mirror grows dark:
if you can see the face
of the full moon
you will be blessed—

if all you can see
is a circle,
you will wander in exile
until it's time
to return—

but if the mirror has grown dark,
close your eyes
before it's too late
and consult the seer
within.

LAILAH

for Laya Firestone-Seghi

When the moon has grown ripe
enough,
she brings forth your wandering soul
and commands it
to enter
the seed.

Midwife of souls,
she watches over you,
and by the light that shines within
reads the long history
of your soul
from the book of dreams.

Sometimes
you remember her
whispering in the dark,
until her words
are imprinted
on every cell.

Sometimes
you hear her voice
just before waking,
guiding your soul
as it threads its way
back.

WIND CHIMES

They play
when the spirit moves them,
rousing you.

Even now
the wind draws its breath
back and forth,

inventing this music
for the first time
and the last.

GHOSTS REHEARSING THE PAST

Waking at night,
another dream world abandoned,
the last images
swirling through my fingers
like sand,
the darkness indecipherable,
all the mirrors grown
dark.

In that dark reflection
I see myself
surrounded by shadows,
all I have forgotten,
ghosts rehearsing the past.

Even now
the family is gathering,
all the voices lost in mourning,
whispers so faint
not even a dream
remembers.

THE BLACK DOLPHIN

in memory of Donald Finkel

There is a black dolphin
swimming in the these waters
with us.
If you submerge,
you will hear its song
rising up
from within.

Yes,
the dolphin is diving
below.

Even now
it's searching for new songs,
each one another pearl
recovered
from the waters
of oblivion.

What other purpose do we serve
but to build a barrier
against eternity,
a fragile coral reef
of song?

A HANDFUL OF SCATTERED SPARKS

First
you must find
a handful
of scattered sparks.

Know
they could be anywhere,
disguised as fallen stars,
under the dark side of a leaf,
in a hollow shell,
or glimmering
in a dark pool.

Too often you return
with an empty sack
slung over your shoulder.
This time
bring back
a netful of scattered sparks.

Take them out,
hold them in your hands.

Remember
how to contain them,
how to keep them
from igniting
until they are
ripe.

Keep your hands closed
like a cauldron,

wait until you can see
with the eye in your hand
a vision of the broken vessels
still scattering
their sparks.

When the sparks begin to throb
like a golden bird,
let go,
set them free,
scatter them all over
again.

TREE OF LIFE

The smallest branches
break off
on their own
and come alive,
crawling toward the dark
waters.
Soon
there are clusters
of tiny fish
filling the depths,
a shimmering cloud
rising up from below,
breaking free of the waters,
a flock of sparrows
taking flight.

IV

GATHERING THE SPARKS

(1979)

BLESSING OF THE FIRSTBORN

for Tsila

Like new waters that form nightly,
we embrace
the breath of the beginning
with arms
of air
and submerge
in these waters of the moon
to receive the blessing
of the firstborn,
whose seed
has taken root
inside you,
whose ark
has been set adrift
in this world,
whose pool is replenished
in caverns of sleep
by the waters that swirl around us,
before the circle they inscribe
becomes a full moon
at rest.

PSALM

Father,
you are the trunk,
we are the branches.
When the Ark opens,
we stand beside your silver tree
on this side of the earth
reading your words
over and over,
raking the coals.

And when we look up
and glimpse the future
lashed to the mast of an ark,
rolling over the waters
of a dark sea,
we wrap ourselves
once more
in your garment of light,
your prayer shawl
woven from the fabric
of history.

But father,
we are still waiting
for the rain that must come
on its own,
and for the tree that will spring up
out of those waters
and bear fruit.

GATHERING THE SPARKS

Long before the sun cast a shadow,
before the word was spoken
that brought the heavens
and the earth
into being,
a flame emerged
from a single,
unseen point,
and from the center of this flame
sparks of light sprang forth,
concealed in shells,
that set sail everywhere,
above
and below,
like a fleet of ships,
each carrying its cargo
of light.

Somehow,
no one knows why,
the frail vessels broke open,
split asunder,
and all the sparks were scattered
like sand
like seeds
like stars.

That is why we were created—
to search for those sparks
no matter where they have been hidden,
and as each one is revealed,
to be consumed
in our own fire
and reborn

out of our own
ashes.

Someday,
when the sparks have been gathered,
the vessels will be restored,
and the fleet will set sail
across another ocean
of space,
and the word will be spoken
again.

ANGELS IN THE TREE

They can only be seen
at sunset:

one whose sleep is filled
with moons,

one whose song grows dark in you,
crying,

one
who sits at the center,

holding the heavens
to the earth—

and one
who is waiting for you to fly

from your body and float
beside blossoms

drifting like prayers
in every direction.

AN ORCHESTRA OF ANGELS

for David Halperin

If you go outside late at night
and listen carefully,
you may hear
an ethereal music drifting down
from an orchestra
of angels.

Those who have heard them
marvel at how long
they are able to hold their notes,
drawing their breath
back and forth
like the ancient one himself,
who in this way
brought the heavens and earth
into being.

The score of this symphony
is the scroll of the Torah,
commencing with the long note of the letter *bet,*
endless and eternal,
each instrument playing in turn
as it appears on the page,
holding its note until the next is sounded,
then breathing in and out,
a full breath.

Some say
the world only exists
so that these harmonies
can be heard.

ISCAH

Rabbi Isaac observed: Iscah was Sarah,
and why was she called Iscah? Because
she foresaw the future by divine inspiration.
—The Talmud

She is the dark sister
standing in the shadow
of the cave,
who peers into the bonfire
burning within.

Sometimes
she accompanies you
with her instrument,
sometimes
she lets you pray
with her voice,
or share
the sound of her breathing,
or even
her song.

This time
she lets you read
your lifeline
as if the words were already
written.

If only
you would kneel by the fire,
she whispers,
you would understand
why no water
can extinguish

this flame—
why all the logs burst into buds
and all the kinds of wood
put forth
fruit.

ANTIDOTES

When the rock refuses your thirst,
raise your staff
and strike it,
and if it opens to you,
take care
not to let its waters
go to waste.

When the pond becomes an empty bowl,
abandon it.
Instead,
gather firewood,
so that if lightning strikes,
there will be something left
to burn.

When the fire has grown cold,
dig in the earth
until you come to the symbols
inscribed
on potsherds
buried deep
in the ashes.

ANATH

in memory of Anath Bental

Anath—
the farmer and his son are desolate.

They could not keep you from sleeping
under the ice.

The surface
of that glacial pool

had not been broken
since the roof of the Temple

was torn down.
They had no rope with them.

The one they made out of clothing
broke.

The son went for help
but it was too late.

The farmer
didn't know the language

you spoke at the end.

TREE OF SOULS

All souls are suspended
like sleeping infants
in so many
cradles.

They alone
hear the long note
rising up from the roots,
the song
echoing in the branches
of the tree.

They alone
see the aura surrounding the tree
like the faint flame
of a burning
bush.

THESE TWO

The question is
how to overhear
the angels
as they whisper
among themselves:

Forty days
before they were born,
it was revealed
that these two,
whose souls are like twin stars,
shall meet
and be married
in a city that is itself
a bride.

I tell you
I have heard them,
and I have heard the spirits
of sons and daughters
still unborn
begging me to take care,
take care that the nest does not
burn down.

Somehow
we must learn how to read
the letters written
in the stars that circle
our souls.

BLACK PEARL

Sometimes
when the sunset has been saved
for the darkness
to grow in,
she shelters me
where the voice of the waterfall
mingles
with that of the waves.

If only
we could follow this refrain,
we could cross
to the other side,
where a black pearl can be seen
glowing like a dark sun
at the bottom of a well.

There
we would dive down
together,
breath suspended like a long note,
and emerge
with a pearl
in our possession,
held between us
like a crystal
cup.

GENESIS

Long ago,
when the world was so new
rain had not yet fallen,
three angels gathered in a garden
around a well,
and one by one they drew water
and poured it out
into vessels of wood,
and clay,
and stone.

From the wood grew a tree
that gave birth to a woman
who grew ripe,
and from the clay
they formed the features
of the first man to see her face,
and from the stone they carved a seat,
and sat back for centuries,
watching.

SHIRA

A white bird,
half human,
whose wings in flight
echo the crystal music
of the stars,
she descends into my sleep,
blessing my voice,
my name,
the letters of the kingdom,
even the crown.

A white bird,
winged messenger,
whose feathers are woven
of moon rays,
whose heart
is a living opal,
she rises to the surface
from the cradle of the seed,
rocked in the waters
of the womb.

A white bird,
sister of my soul,
she balances between
the stars above
and the stars
below.
There
we rock in each other's arms,
one of us sleeping,
one always
awake.

ABRAHAM IN EGYPT

There was a famine in the land;
and Abraham went down into Egypt to sojourn there,
for the famine was sore in the land.
—Genesis 12:10

I came to the desert
too soon.
There nothing flourished
but the twin herbs of fear
and despair,
and there was nothing
to guide me,
for my fire was out.

Still
I kept watch
and so I saw a white bird flying toward me
that dropped a tiny seed at my feet—
and I cradled it,
and kneaded the earth to make it ready,
and planted it
while the seed was still damp
from its source.

That is how
white blossoms came to appear
and soon there was a single fruit.
And when I broke it open,
I found as many seeds as stars,
and when I tasted it,
I drank from the spring that winds within
and followed it as far as I could,
knowing it would lead me
out of Egypt.

HOW THE TENTH TRIBE LOST ITS WORDS

For years after separating from their brothers,
the tenth lost tribe paused at dusk,
raised up their tents,
and assembled for the holy services.
But in the thirty-ninth year,
they could not agree on where to seek
the promised land.

Soon after,
when they assembled for prayer,
no words sang out,
for they had lost the word
open,
and from that day on,
the scroll remained tightly closed.

Divining the fate this sign foretold,
the prophets so frightened the people,
no man dared lie with his wife.
Instead they stretched out alone and discovered
the silence of their empty hands,
and by morning they had lost the word
hold.

Soon their wanderings were cut short.
Day after day they stayed in their tents
and refused to continue their journey.
At last they agreed among themselves
that this place was their home,
and that day they lost the word
search.

Before long not only the people,
but the animals, the birds

and even the winds had grown silent.
Within a year no one could speak
the ancient tongue;
its words were scattered through the desert
like clouds of dust.

THE BLACK SWAN

First,
you must enter a seashell
and find where the sea is hidden.
Wait there
until your eyes can discern shadows,
then draw your breath backward,
dive below,
and release the black swan.

She will rise up from her cradle,
unfold her wings,
prepare to fly,
in her beak a black pearl,
a seed ready to take root,
a dream song
growing ripe.

V

VESSELS

(1977)

OUR ANGELS

in memory of Yehuda Amichai

Our angels
spend much of their time sleeping.
In their dreams
they tear down the new houses by the sea
and build old ones
in their place.

No matter how long they may sleep,
one hundred, two hundred years—
ten centuries is not too much—
the first to wake up
takes the torch that has been handed down,
adds a drop of oil to the lamp,
blesses the eternal light,
and then recalls the name
of every other angel,
and one by one as they are remembered
they wake up.

For them
as for us
there is nothing more beautiful
than memory.

ADAM'S DREAM

The blossoms closed into buds
singing only to themselves.
The sweet hand that guarded my heart
stirred within my body.
I reached for you as you pulled away
and followed the arm's length
that linked us. I could hear
the dark pools filling, the breath you took
rising over the waters.
I felt the life leave me
with a gasp that gave me life.
No eyes opened to ask or to answer,
yet then I knew you were another
that I had lost,
that you would never remember
why the wound couldn't heal itself
once we had awakened.

ABRAHAM

When the last outnumber
the first,
he is the sad father
who wanders in exile.

His sons,
the sentinels,
worship boundaries
in a land without memory,

his daughters,
the slaves,
mourn in the mirrors
at dusk.

SARAH

She prays
like the water,
waiting as a wave to be formed.
Somewhere in the highest branches
she restores herself
in silence.
Spirit, voice, not yet a word,
she enters where the moons change
and shows me
a door standing open,
a star taking root
in the branches of a tree.
Like a singer surrendering her voice,
she offers me
the question
in her hand.

What I had
to give her
is gone.

ISAAC

It was there one day at dusk.
I looked up
and saw a body of light that was an angel
take its place in the branches of that tree.
I looked away at once,
and when I raised my eyes
there was nothing more
than the dark regret of leaves
longing for that light.

Even then I was never certain
I had really seen an angel,
but when we turned to go,
a path cleared beneath the moon,
and silence called its secret from the forest
with the wings of a hidden flock.

THE RIVER GODDESS

She sleeps
to the sound of her own breathing,
her voice,
the quiet surface before the falls,
her song,
a long note rising out of water.

All night
the rivers of her hands
are crossed with currents,
each hand
a white shell cracked in fire,
a dark sea
that cannot be named.

There,
in caverns of sleep,
her instrument is her voice,
the sound of her breathing,
her song,
the dream of a river
searching for
the sea.

A DREAM OF DEPARTURE

All down the narrow, winding path
her eyes are fixed
on the stars that crowd the sky.
Sometimes she seems reluctant
to continue, and rests
at each new turn,
but still
she does not look back.

Her progress is very slow,
but at last she reaches
a river,
almost hidden in the darkness.
Beside the shore she finds
a boat, its hull
fashioned from jewels.

She casts off in silence;
an unseen current guides her course.
Before I wake
she sails beyond my sight
forever.

THE ALPHABET MUSEUM

for David Meltzer

Perhaps
you were expecting
glass cases filled with parchment,
ancient script,
careful charts hard to comprehend,
a map of constellations,
scrolls, runes,
fragments,
forgotten words,
the key
to a kabbalistic code.

This door
is the stone tablet
you have sought so long.

But the key itself
is too well worn.
Long ago
it turned in the lock
for the last time.

MAPS

At night all the maps grow blank.
First the rocks wear away,
the footholds,
the warpaths,
each and every sacred pool.
Trees are uprooted;
one by one
every province is eclipsed.

All the while
snow can be seen
stealing roses from mounds,
memories from cold stone,
carrying off the last lake
between two mountains.
Before long,
one beach imposes itself
on every other,
one tide returns crest above crest.

When all the oceans are uncharted,
the earth is a glowing coal.
Seen from a distance,
our planet inscribes
a circle,
burning into a blank page
the incandescent outline
of an eclipse.

THE DEMON AWAKE

1.
Filled with darkness,
he is held from sleep,
trapped between dreaming and waking,
or perhaps as was Moses,
having reached sight of his land,
denied.

2.
Another walks beside him,
repeating the stages he has not been spared.
His voice becomes dangerous.
He stops walking.
In the night, stiff and unfamiliar,
a tree reflects a shadow of frost.

3.
The light is cold; coldly he circles,
growing white. One, two,
the last: the cold turning
stops.

THE GOLEM

The circle closes before and behind.
—Sefer Yetsirah

None would bless my presence.
None saw more than what had been
or what would be.

None asked to know my name.
None sought a secret
at the level of my eyes.

None saw the word engraved.
None reached for me
when I fell back to the beginning.

THE SOUND OF TEARING

for Lucien Stryk

Even now,
while you are reading these words,
a dark woman
stands behind you,
tearing these pages
to pieces.

Already
the silence between syllables
has been broken,
the sound of tearing
rises around you,
you build the walls higher and higher,
but the silence cannot be saved.

Nothing,
not all the forests
that scatter their seeds
in circles,
can restore those pages
fallen at her feet.

RECKONING

For every dark cloud, a red warning.

For every blade brighter than the sun,
an animal clawing
the darkness.

For every wounded tree,
a dark sun dropping out of the sky.

THE TRAPPED

With darkness, their only element,
they must create caves,
hollow mountains
to contain the offerings
no fire can consume.

When the caves are completed
they abandon them
like fallen skins

and burrow further
into the mouth of darkness.

THE TWIN

In the mirror your twin sister,
lacking birth and name,
suffers her jealous confinement.

Raped often by demons,
she regards with bitter humor
the darkness surrounding
your forehead,
that cold lovers push aside
to discover
your naked twin.

During the day
she beckons,
but at night,
torn from sleep,
you find yourself imprisoned,
trapped at the entrance
of her dream,
in the rooms thrown back
upon themselves
like the last of those infinite mirrors,
her eyes.

LOST MYTH OF ALBASHAD

His siren
his father of fever
his barren birth

His needs without names

His orphan
slipping away
lost beneath layers of ice

What remains
when no dream remembers?

Not even a crack not even
a crack not even
a crack.

CONTAINMENT

Anyone can create a bamboo garden in the world,
but who can incorporate the world into his
bamboo grove?
—Hermann Hesse

When the world has lost
another sun

and I cannot contain
the darkness
before it spills inside,

each simple shoot
dons the mask
it has concealed,

each forking path
pulls further apart,

the boundaries
of the circle
cannot find the center.

and no covenant
can restrain
the flood.

IN THE ANCIENT DAYS

In the ancient days there were warnings—
boils,
birthmarks,
a black cloud of locusts.
There was time enough
to paint a sign in blood
on the doorpost,
time to hold your breath
while the angel was passing over.

But now we know nothing of signs.
There is only a great silence
from each of our separate houses,
restless dreams
in the middle of the night,
an invisible presence
like a body about to appear in a coffin,
a glimpse of a hand
or face.

Once angels called out to us
from heaven.
Now they have all disappeared,
along with the patriarchs
who visited our tents.
All that remains
is a memory of wings,
and a sleep that lasts
for centuries.

LYRIC AND LAMENT

for Helene Gottesmann

Last time
we met in a synagogue
somewhere in the Northern circle.
I had been living in a lighthouse,
keeping watch over the waves.
You were waiting for an old man
with white hair
who had promised to come back.
Someone lit a torch.
The flame reflected in the windows,
both doors flew open,
and the wind blew in
great sheaves of paper
that scattered around us
like leaves.
While I watched
you reached out
and caught one in each hand,
a lyric and lament,
two perfect poems.

This time
we met in the desert.
You were crawling in the sand
to Masada.
I was searching for something
to quench my thirst.
A single crow circled in the sky.
What was it you were looking for
in the sand?
Your hands dug out a golden object,
a lamp buried so many centuries,
and inside it
a light with no source
but itself.

OFFERING

in memory of Chris Von Laue

To pray, as the sun is held in a clasp of darkness,
before the seed is wrested from your sleep,

and nearing the altar, to hear the sound
approaching from behind

and see at the same instant, against the snowy hillside,
a bare, sprouting tree—

is to welcome the fire
swelling suddenly at your feet,

to welcome,
beneath a sky open and opening,

one whose hands have touched your sleep
and embrace you now, open as hours.

THE MINYAN

for Bernice

All that year,
before the sun set
and after,
I saw her standing alone
outside the chapel.
It was said that for years
she had not spoken a word
to anyone.

Although
she could not be counted
in the minyan,
the old men believed she came back
to hear them pray Kaddish,
as did the father
who had never stopped mourning
for his son.

Afternoon and evening,
she offered all our prayers
her silence,
and when they ended,
we knew,
by the aura surrounding her face,
if our prayers had ascended
or not.

LULLABY

It's raining.
The torrents weave a girl
kissing me. We follow the flow
from rising springs
into the river, fresh as we surface,
into the sea, sky,
pouring down mountains, arms.
It's snowing.
We part, our kiss frozen.
I climb a hill, slipping backward.
Snow packs between my arms;
the wind stiffens, ices,
the world frozen,
asleep.

LOVE POEM

She coils her body around me,
coils one leg
around my waist.
My hands form the soft clay of her body,
search for her center,
give her hands
a home.
My mouth pauses at more than one place.

Eyes closed,
we know nothing of darkness,
of the river that runs through our sleep.
Coiled inside
a seashell,
the voice of the falls
sounds our sleep
until parted from our dreams.

Her hands sleep between us
like warm birds,
share the heat of folded wings.
Her nipples ask for nothing more
than my mouth,
the words of my tongue.

The earth grows full again,
a blossom breaks open
between us,
more than one moon tears free
untold longing,
illumined from below.

THE NEW YEAR FOR TREES

for Shlomo and Hava Vinner

All year
they have kept a careful record
of everything—
the waters of the moon,
the slow descent
of every sun.
All year
they have charted the course of every comet,
eyes drawn to the center,
to the star that supports
the planet,
the beam that holds up every arch,
the line that continues into the future
unbroken
unchanged.

But tonight,
as the light descends into sleep,
the trees
all lift their branches to the sky,
cradling the moon,
for the first blossoms have appeared
to announce
that all fruit that follows
belongs to the new year
to come.

ORACLE

in memory of Bob Dyer

Six planets
of light and darkness
emerge from a single unseen point.
I enter
a forest I had forgotten.
There I am
father of the elements,
of the image.
I open my hand
and see the characters,
too blurred to be read.
I dream of a child,
an orphan
I saved from a fire.
I dream of a river
that winds
within.
I focus
on the words of the oracle,
and line by line
bring them into
being.

VESSELS

for Tsila

We, too, were created from clay
mined from a cavern
or the bottom of a dark pool,
shaped by the hand of a father
and mother
and blessed
with the breath of life,
that light that shines through us
like a small sun
concealed in the embryo
of an egg.

We too are vessels,
baked in the sun by day,
filled with the light of the moon
at night.
This moonlight
has taken root inside us,
has given us this bright glaze.
It's our memory of the shadow
of many pale hands
waiting for us to grow ripe enough
to receive.

To receive
and to transmit,
to grow transparent
in the hour of the offering,
the sacred time
between two ceremonies,
when, at last,
the pool can be replenished,
when you walk around me
seven times
and I begin to glow.

A SONG

A song
that seemed so brief at first
has lasted,
the fire living in your hands
still mingles in mine.
Like wood near water
I'm an old poplar sprouting at the root,
whose branches would burn
in your fire,
whose seasons would find shelter
in your house of song.
For the wind that blows between us
speaks also to the spark
that clings to me like a prayer—
a dream that shapes shadows
into moons
that settle to the surface
like perfect pools
of light—
that haunts my buds into blossom,
my voice
into song.

RUTH

So she lay at his feet until morning.
Ruth 3:14

Just before midnight I opened my eyes
and found her asleep on the threshing-floor
beside me.
She had slipped beneath the blanket
and was sleeping
at my feet.
Then, gently as I could,
I lifted her out from under the cover,
until her head came to rest on the straw
next to mine,
and I lay there beside her
all night,
her head in the hollow of my shoulder,
until she departed at dawn.

THE PRAYERS

for Mary Ann Steiner

There is the prayer of the father of rain,
the prayer of the golden coin
buried in a black box,
all the prayers in the cracks in the Wall,
marked down one by one,
sorted out,
waiting to be heard.

Then there are the prayers
of all the sunsets never seen,
prayers closed like sleeping flowers,
prayers whose fire
is forgotten, whose darkness
is not enough.

Listen—
there is also the prayer of the daughter
who waits for the seasons like a tree,
her wishes silent,
and the prayer of the son
who waits for the fruit to fall,
for the seeds to break open
in the earth.

These are the prayers
the angels take up together,
that fuse to form the prayer of the child
they receive in return,
who brings these words back
with a blessing
from the dark sun
of their source.

LYRIC

I sing whispering
into the thin ear
out of the dark.

Heat trails long,
the hollow complete
sun sets inside.

A BLESSING

Now, while she sleeps
on your arm,
lie back.
You have been blessed.
Your sleep is assured.
You will awake
rested.

Now, while the curtain is closed,
while you wait for the constellation
of two mouths,
draw your breath backward,
let your body fall to the floor
to sleep,
let your eyes look inward
at the face the moon forms
out of the dark.

Already twilight is coming closer.
Soon a red sun will rise,
soon you will be given
a second chance
to secure the seed,
to carry it further,
into sleep.

Now, while there is still time,
let this nameless star
take its place
inside you.
No goddess could refuse
a silence ready for harvest
and the ripe sun
in your throat.

CALLING THE MOON CLOSER

All at once
I find her taking root
in the soft earth beside me.
It's hard to wake her.
Even when her eyes are open
she cannot decide
how to breathe—
whether to draw her breath
like a young girl
or let her leaves absorb
the light.
Still
she calls the moon closer,
and lets me hold her
in my arms,
and all the while she shelters me,
the branches are filled
with a silver light,
as if the moon had slipped
inside.

NOTES

"Genealogy"
This poem combines a kabbalistic creation myth found in the *Zohar* with modern cosmological theory.

"Manna"
In Exodus 16:4-36 God provided food, called manna, for the Israelites in the wilderness by raining it down from heaven. There was no need to cook or bake it. God commanded them to collect it daily, except on Friday, when they were to gather a double portion, since no work is permitted on the Sabbath.

"Dolphin Songs"
Dolphins are mammals, which means that at some point they lived on the land and later returned to the sea. No one knows why they abandoned the land for the sea.

"Her Palette"
Marjorie Stelmach's books of poetry include *Night Drawings, A History of Disappearance*, and *Bent Upon Light*.

"The Interpreter"
This poem was inspired by a solo violin sonata by Heinrich von Biber.

"The Last Reading"
Donald Finkel (1929-2008) was a prominent poet and teacher of poetry writing at Washington University in St. Louis. His books include *A Joyful Noise, A Mote in Heaven's Eye,* and *What Manner of Beast.*

"Grandfathers"
My mother's father was William Rubin (1898-1968). My father's father was Charles Schwartz (1886-1956).

"Grebenes"
My grandmother was Lena Schwartz (1898-1965). *Grebenes* was a popular food of Eastern European Jews, made from chicken skin fried in schmaltz, chicken fat.

"The Lost Film"
The film was shot by our cousin, Ben Friedman, in 1944. The section of the film involving my family lasts about five minutes.

"Dreams About My Father"
My father was Nathan Schwartz (1916-1973).

"Dreams About My Mother"
My mother was Bluma Schwartz (1923-2005).

"Escape Artist"
My wife, Tsila Schwartz, specializes in traditional Jewish art, such as *ketubot* (Jewish wedding contracts) and amulets.

"Maury Has Slipped Away"
Maury Schwartz (1927-2011) was my father's younger brother.

"Adam's Soul"
Many rabbinic legends (midrashim) assert that Adam's soul contained all souls.

"The Tree of Life and the Tree of Death"
In *Folklore in the Old Testament*, James Frazer theorizes that the original myth of the two trees in Genesis was likely about the Tree of Life and the Tree of Death, not about the Tree of Life and the Tree of Knowledge, and that it was a myth about the origin of death, not about disobedience to God.

"Gifts"
In the midrash, the fig is said to have been the forbidden fruit, and Adam and Eve used fig leaves to cover themselves after they realized they were naked. The mandrake root was believed to be an aphrodisiac. Jewish folk tradition views the pomegranate as a symbol of fertility.

"Before You Were Born"
I first heard the myth of the angel Lailah from my mother when I was a child.

"The Golem Speaks"
In Jewish folklore, the golem is a man made from clay who is brought to life by kabbalistic magic in order to protect Jews from the Blood Libel, an accusation that triggered many pogroms in Eastern Europe. The golem could not speak or reproduce and had to follow the commands of the rabbi who created him.

"The Last Time I Saw Lilith"
In Jewish folklore Lilith was Adam's first wife, who abandoned him and became, eventually, the Queen of Demons.

"Why is Isaac Missing?"
At the end of Genesis 22, only Abraham is said to come down from Mount Moriah. The mystery of Isaac's absence fascinated the rabbis.

"The Spice of the Sabbath"
This is based on a medieval Jewish legend found in *Ma'aseh me-ha-hayyat*.

"People of the Stories"
The Jewish people are known as the People of the Book, but they are just as well the People of the Stories, since they brought their stories with them. These stories take place in eternal, sacred time.

"Jacob Never Died"
A midrash asserts that Jacob never died, despite the clear depiction of his death in Genesis 49:33.

"I Breathed In"
This poem was inspired by the kabbalistic theory of *tzimtzum*, asserting that God contracted Himself prior to the creation of the world to make space for creation.

"The Calling"
A speculative poem about how Rabbi Isaac Luria came to create the myth of the shattering of the vessels and the gathering of the sparks.

"Confession"
Rabbi Nachman of Bratslav is widely regarded as the greatest Jewish storyteller.

"Dreams About Reb Zalman"
Rabbi Zalman Schachter-Shalomi is the beloved founder of the Renewal movement in Judaism. His books include *A Hidden Light* and *A Heart Afire: Stories and Teachings of the Early Hasidic Masters*.

"Tashlikh"
A popular Jewish custom of emptying one's pockets before Rosh Hashanah, the new year, as a symbolic means of casting away one's sins.

"Before and After"
Mishnah Hagigah 2:1 states that anyone who asks what came before or what will come after, or what is above and what is below—would have been better off never to have been born.

"Jung's Dream"
C.G. Jung reports this dream in *Memories, Dreams, Reflections*.

"Dreams About Borges"
The great Argentine writer Jorge Luis Borges has become, like Franz Kafka, a mythic figure in our time and a presence in my dreams.

"The Dancer"
Forty year ago, when I worked in a hospital, I overheard a young woman recount these dreams to a friend, as she descended a stairway behind me.

"A Photo of Gombrowicz"
Witold Gombrowicz (1929-1969) was a prominent Polish novelist.

"Memories of the Alhambra"
"Memories of the Alhambra" is a classical guitar piece composed in 1896 by the Spanish composer Francisco Tarrega. Lyle Harris (1933-2011) was a master of classical and jazz guitar.

"A Palace of Bird Beaks"
A kind of *Ars Poetica*.

II BREATHING IN THE DARK

"Breathing in the Dark"
The angel who whispers to the unborn child is Lailah, the angel of conception in Jewish lore. She is said to guard the child in the womb and to read from the Book of Secrets.

"A Letter to My Uncle Howard"
Howard Rubin (1914-1942) lost his life when his ship was bombed in World War II.

"Inheritance"
Two stories, about the angel Lailah and the demoness Lilith, have become touchstones for me. Lailah is said to touch the lips of the newborn child as if to say *shhh*. This is the folk explanation for the mysterious indentation on everyone's upper lip.

"A Portrait of My Son"
Challah is a braided bread used for Sabbath blessings. The *shuk* is a market.

"Spirit Guide"
Savta is Hebrew for grandmother. Miriam's grandmother was Rachel Khanem of Jerusalem, who died October 1, 2002.

"Afterlife"
The last stanza describes a kind of positive spiritual possession in Judaism, known as possession by *ibbur*. An *ibbur* is the spirit of a wise person who has died, whose spirit fuses with a living man.

"Ava"
This poem is based on a dream I had in Sarasota, Florida, on May 24, 2007. My granddaughter, Ava, was born on June 1, 2007.

"Signs of the Lost Tribe"

Jewish folklore recounts that ten of the twelve tribes of Israel vanished. No one knows what happened to them. Many peoples, such as the Ethiopian Jews, claim to be descended from one of the lost tribes.

"A Wall Rubbing"

The Wall is the *Kotel,* the Western Wall in Jerusalem, last retaining wall of the Temple that was destroyed in 70 C.E. It is also known as the Wailing Wall.

"The Tomb of the Ari"

Rabbi Isaac Luria, known as the Ari, lived in Safed in northern Israel in the 16th century and is buried there. He is widely regarded as the greatest Jewish mystic.

"Songs of Nazine"

The core dream that inspired this poem is the last section.

"Swimming to Jerusalem"

According to Jewish lore, when the Messiah comes, the bones of the righteous will roll through enchanted caves to the Mount of Olives in Jerusalem, where they will be resurrected.

"The Hidden Light"

This poem is based on a midrash about the light of the first day.

"The First Eve"

Most rabbinic legends identify Lilith as Adam's first wife, but a few speak of the first Eve, who was created before his eyes, while he was awake.

"Lilith's Cave"

In rabbinic lore, Lilith, Adam's first wife, left him and took up residence in a cave by the Red Sea. Later Lilith, already a child-strangling witch and the incarnation of lust, also became identified as the Queen of Demons. She is said to be warded off with a *hamsa,* an amulet of a hand with a watchful eye in the center of it.

"Cain"

See Genesis 4:1-16.

"River Dream"

See Exodus 1-10.

"Out of Egypt"

This poem was inspired by a midrash about how some of the enslaved Israelites were reluctant to leave Egypt.

"The Angel of Losses"
This is based on a teaching of Rabbi Nachman of Bratslav, who identified this angel as Yod'ea, which means *he knows*.

"Two Meditations"
These two poems are based on kabbalistic meditative exercises.

"Dreams About Kafka"
All sections of this poem were drawn from my dream journal, and are actual dreams about Franz Kafka.

"City of the Dead"
Rabbi Arnold Asher (1935-1978) was a beloved and respected congregational rabbi in St. Louis who died at 43. Five thousand mourners attended his funeral.

"Kaddish on a Bridge"
Leon Hereid (1953-1994) was married to my cousin Judy at the time of his sudden death.

"The Library of Dreams"
In "The Aleph," Borges describes an Aleph, a glowing point of light in which it is possible to see everything in the world simultaneously. Samuel Taylor Coleridge wrote "Kubla Khan" in an opium dream, but before he could finish writing it down, a man from Porlock interrupted him, and when he returned to the poem, he had forgotten the rest of it.

"Singing Bones"
See Ezekiel 37, the vision of the valley of dry bones.

"A Vision"
In the vision, the wall of the room disappeared and I saw an exceptionally beautiful beach.

"The Last Sunset"
Gabriel Preil (1911-1993) was a Hebrew poet who spent most of his life in New York, where he was largely unknown, with occasional visits to Israel, where he was highly acclaimed. He died in Jerusalem on June 5, 1993.

"Yehuda Amichai in the Heavenly Jerusalem"
Yehuda Amichai (1924-2000) was the greatest modern Israeli poet. Rabbinic and kabbalistic lore describe a heavenly Jerusalem, the mirror image of the earthly Jerusalem.

"Miriam's Well"
According to rabbinic lore, God created an enchanted well in honor of Miriam, sister of Moses, that followed the Israelites in the wilderness, providing them with fresh water.

"Mermaids"
Mermaids and Sirens are polar opposites in sea lore, positive and negative feminine mythic figures of the sea.

"The Covenant of the Stars"
This poem reflects my ambivalence about Judaism—a reluctance to observe Jewish law and ritual, combined with a fascination with Jewish tradition. The ending alludes to Martin Buber's *I and Thou*.

"The Dark Orchard"
Inspired by the famous talmudic passage about the four who entered Paradise in B. Haggiah 14b. Three of the four rabbis were hurt as a result of their mystical ascent: Ben Azzai looked and died; Ben Zoma looked and lost his mind; Elisha ben Abuyah became an apostate; and only Rabbi Akiba entered and departed in peace. I devoted a short novel, *The Four Who Entered Paradise*, to this enigmatic passage.

"Salt"
Some years ago I ran a computer program, which listed the number of times a word appeared in a text, on my dream journal, in order to identify my obsessions. To my surprise, the word that appeared at the top of the list was *salt*. I did a search and discovered a very long dream about salt. I condensed it into this poem, one of my favorites.

"Courting Oblivion"
This poem began as a migraine headache. As soon as I wrote it down, the headache disappeared.

"Lailah"
Lailah is the angel of conception. I first heard this Jewish myth from my mother. See "Before You Were Born."

"The Cave of the Four Winds"
Based on a medieval myth from the Hebrew folktale "The Prince of Coucy," this is a proto-atomic warning myth, as if nuclear weapons had been anticipated.

"Oracle of the Oil"
Using oil in this fashion is an ancient method of divination.

"A Handful of Scattered Sparks"
Based on Rabbi Isaac Luria's (known as the Ari) 16th century myth about the shattering of the vessels and the gathering of the sparks. See "Gathering the Sparks."

IV GATHERING THE SPARKS (1979)

"Gathering the Sparks"
This poem retells Rabbi Isaac Luria's myth of the shattering of the vessels and the gathering of the sparks. See my book *Tree of Souls: The Mythology of Judaism*, pp. 122-124.

"Iscah"
The name Iscah appears in the difficult genealogy of Abraham and Sarah in Genesis 11:29. In rabbinic sources Iscah was identified as Sarah when she turned to her prophetic side. See *B. Sanhedrin* 69b.

"Anath"
Anath Bental (1950-1975) was an Israeli poet and good friend of mine who drowned in 1975 at 25 in Norway when the glacier she was crossing split open.

"Tree of Souls"
At the time I wrote this poem in 1978, I had no idea that I would use the title for my book of Jewish mythology, *Tree of Souls*, published in 2004.

"These Two"
This poem responds to a rabbinic belief found in the Talmud (B. Sota 2a) that *Forty days before the formation of a child, a voice goes forth out of heaven to announce that this one will marry that one. And each match is as difficult for the Holy One to arrange as was the dividing of the Red Sea.*

"Shira"
I wrote this poem shortly after the birth of my first child, Shira, in 1978.

"How the Tenth Tribe Lost Its Words"
According to Jewish legend, ten of the twelve tribes of Israel vanished from history. There are all sorts of theories about what happened to them.

V VESSELS (1977)

"Abraham"
This was my first poem about Abraham. It tries to convey the presence—and absence—of the patriarch in modern Israel.

"Sarah"
This was my first poem about the muse, here identified as the matriarch Sarah. It took six months to complete it.

"Isaac"
This poem was inspired by the belief that I had glimpsed an angel in a park.

"The Alphabet Museum"
This poem was inspired by David Meltzer's account of his visit to just such a museum.

"The Demon Awake"
This poem is based on the earliest dream I recorded in my dream journal in 1965.

"The Golem"
In Jewish folklore a golem is a man made out of clay and brought to life with kabbalistic magic. See "The Golem Speaks."

"The Sound of Tearing"
Based on a strange incident I witnessed during a reading of Zen poetry by Lucien Stryk. A woman in the audience stood and tore up the same book Stryk was reading from. See my essay "The Sound of Tearing/The Destroyer of Books" in *Zen, Poetry, the Art of Lucien Stryk*, edited by Susan Porterfield, pp. 211-216.

"Lost Myth of Albashad"
This poem is all that remained of a long dream I had about the myth of Albashad, which largely vanished when I woke up.

"Lyric and Lament"
Based on two dreams recounted to me by Helene Gottesmann, over a period of several years.

"Offering"
I wrote this poem after learning that Chris Von Laue, a young man, had died, for no apparent reason, during a Quaker prayer service.

"The Minyan"
Jewish law requires ten men (a minyan) be present before the service can begin. In recent years non-Orthodox Jews have come to count women in the minyan, but at the time this was written, they did not.

"The New Year for Trees"
The Jewish new year for trees, Tu Beshvat, celebrates the appearance of the first blossoms in spring.

"Oracle"

I have been a student of the *I Ching* for many years. That is the starting point of this poem. Bob Dyer wrote a memorable book of poems about the *I Ching, Oracle of the Turtle.*

"Vessels"

The third stanza refers to a Jewish wedding custom where the bride walks around the groom seven times, binding herself to him. Recently the custom has been modified to have both bride and groom circle each other.

HOWARD SCHWARTZ is the author of five books of poems: *Vessels, Gathering the Sparks, Sleepwalking Beneath the Stars, Breathing in the Dark,* and *The Library of Dreams.* He is also the co-editor (with Anthony Rudolf) of *Voices Within the Ark: The Modern Jewish Poets.* His other books include *Tree of Souls: The Mythology of Judaism,* which won the National Jewish Book Award and *Leaves from the Garden of Eden: One Hundred Classic Jewish Tales.*

CAREN LOEBEL-FRIED is the author and illustrator of *Legend of the Gourd, Lono and the Magical Land Beneath the Sea, Hawaiian Legends of Dreams,* and *Hawaiian Legends of the Guardian Spirits.* She illustrated *Pua Polu, the Pretty Blue Hawaiian Flower,* and *Naupaka,* written by Nona Beamer, and *Tree of Souls,* written by Howard Schwartz. Awards for Caren's books include the American Folklore Society's Aesop Prize for Children's Folklore, the Hawai'i Book Publishers Association Awards for Illustration, Literature, and Hawaiian Culture.